Hudson Valley
WINE

Hudson Valley WINE

A **HISTORY** OF **TASTE** & **TERROIR**

TESSA EDICK AND KATHLEEN WILLCOX

AMERICAN PALATE

Published by American Palate
A Division of The History Press
Charleston, SC
www.historypress.net

First published 2017

Manufactured in the United States

ISBN 9781467119764

Library of Congress Control Number: 2017938329

Notice: The information in this book is true and complete to the best of our knowledge. It is offered without guarantee on the part of the authors or The History Press. The authors and The History Press disclaim all liability in connection with the use of this book.

his lips drink water but his heart drinks wine
—e.e. cummings

For all of us with a food dream and a commitment to local agriculture.

CONTENTS

INTRODUCTION

$\mathcal{T}$he Hudson Valley holds bragging rights as the birthplace of American wine.

If you did not know, you are not alone.

Agriculture is New York State's economic engine, and grapes fuel that engine. The New York grape, grape juice and wine industry produces more than $4.8 billion in economic benefits annually. Only two states produce more grapes than New York State: California and Washington.

"The craft beverage industry is one of New York's greatest success stories, and we are doing everything we can in state government to keep the tremendous growth seen by our wineries, breweries, cideries and distilleries going strong," New York State Governor Andrew Cuomo said. "From Long Island to the Finger Lakes, these local businesses support jobs and economic activity in both agriculture and tourism, and investing in them means investing in New York's future."

Hudson Valley wine, as opposed to wine from the Finger Lakes and Long Island (two New York wine regions finally enjoying much-deserved critical and financial success), is often spurned by critics almost reflexively, leaving many who live and drink here to wonder, *Have they even tried it?*

Over the last century, Hudson Valley wine has not been honored like left coast vintages or even celebrated like counterparts in other areas of the state. As we start to investigate *why*, it becomes clear that the unique terroir of the region may hold the keys to the region's struggles and its eventual ascendancy.

New York Governor Andrew Cuomo and FarmOn! Foundation founder Tessa Edick. *Courtesy of FarmOnFoundation.org.*

The Hudson Valley is a landscape from which artists and farmers in particular have drawn inspiration and sustenance for centuries. It represents everything we love about America: hardworking people, fertile land, a majestic river that roams from the countryside to the city yielding a breadbasket, innovation and fresh air that shapes the freedom we believe is our birthright.

The meadows, the hills, the fields, the orchards and the mountains bend along the Hudson River and inspire people to be responsible, cultivate honest food and explore the best the Hudson River Valley has to offer and the terroir that rewards these practices.

For four centuries, the Hudson Valley terroir has served up some of the country's most coveted vegetables, fruit, grain, dairy, meat, poultry and spirits from seed and soil, and America has responded in kind, making it one of the most beloved destinations in the world, a treasure along the Taconic. Visitors from New York City and beyond flock for the delectable bites, breathtaking landscapes and a pioneer spirit that is tough to replicate and impossible to fake. Like our European ancestors, the key to America's heart is our stomachs, by way of our palates.

The mellowing maritime effect of the Hudson River helps ease the harshness of cold winters and hot summers for vineyards that grow close to its bank. *Courtesy of the Wine and Grape Foundation.*

Locally sourced, honestly made farm-fresh food has commanded attention in the Hudson River Valley region again in the last decade and reinvigorated the agricultural industry with more farm markets, farm stands, Community Supported Agriculture (CSA) programs and farm-to-table restaurants, with eaters and drinkers demanding organic, grass-fed, pastured meats; just-picked local fruit and vegetables; locally grown and produced libations; and other artisanal handcrafted products, all grown and farmed with best practices in mind—be it organic, bio-dynamic or responsibly grown. We are looking for new (old) ways to satisfy our taste buds, fuel our bodies with nutrition from the fertile land and connect us to seed and soil, so that we can once again be celebrated as the breadbasket of America and reassert our historical ties to the country's vibrant wine industry.

In the Hudson Valley, the oft-repeated phrase "know where your food comes from" is a way of life. Often, we take a step further here; we know the farmers who grew it, the patch of land it springs from, the quality and strength of sun's light and the way it changes from fall to winter and spring to summer. We shake the hands that feed us over farmers' market stalls, and we raise a glass of (local) wine *with* them on one of the many local feasting days to celebrate harvests, accomplishments, strife and challenges as a community that stands together.

Hudson Valley wine. *Courtesy of abc kitchen.*

For many local food and libation lovers from afar, the Culinary Institute of America (CIA) is their first foray into the Hudson Valley, which to outsiders can seem intimidatingly spread out and difficult to navigate. It's a great place to start. In addition to being centrally located in Hyde Park near Rhinebeck (home of FDR), the institute has been designed, from the ground up, to celebrate local food and drink. The many restaurants, the cafés and yes, even a brewery, all on campus, teach the next generation of chefs, brewers, winemakers and sommeliers how to help create and maintain the business of food and drink sustainably. The CIA serves as a mecca for many a day-tripping Manhattanite eager to learn more about the Hudson Valley and its multigenerational family farmers, chefs and winemakers who make it such a delicious and beautiful place to visit or live.

The Hudson River Valley runs from the northern cities of Albany and Troy to the southern city of Yonkers along the eastern section of the state; it's nestled in the Appalachian highlands in communities bordering the 315-mile watercourse known as the Hudson River.

The river is named after Henry Hudson, who "discovered" it in 1609 when he sailed up the waterway. The river's history extends further back, of course, to the River Indians, the Mohawk and Munsees, who populated the valley for generations before the arrival of the Europeans, who brought disease, fierce competition for land and war.

The Hudson River slices through the middle of twelve counties, providing water and temperate maritime breezes that soften the sometimes harsh extremes of its weather patterns. During the Ice Age, New York was heavily glaciated, and when the ice melted, we were left with miles of rich, fertile (though rocky) soil, perfect for an enormous variety of flora and fauna. Hudson Valley terroir can support a rotational management of row crops, grain varietals, vegetables, fruit, grazing animals, pollinating bees and butterflies. The yield provides enough bounty and diversity to sustain all of the hungry and thirsty omnivores from New York City to New England and back with seasonal food that is fresh, tastier, more nutrient dense and sustainable, as it has not been shipped in from halfway around the world with a carbon footprint as big as the Empire State.

Once known as the breadbasket of the United States, the Hudson Valley is where we began growing our food as a nation and preserved farmland for food security. Before the first Dutch settlements were established around 1610 at Fort Nassau (just south of Albany), Mohican and Munsee tribes populated the valley, planting fields to complement their diet of readily available fish and game.

After European settlers started arriving, as early as the 1620s, the French Huguenots followed forty years later, fleeing religious persecution. Among many other endeavors, they started vineyards in the area, which means the Hudson Valley is, in fact, one of the oldest winemaking regions in the country.

In the seventeenth century, settlers began building major colony operations, claiming territory from the Delaware River to the Connecticut River and setting up fortified outposts and colonial operations up and down the river, from Fort Orange near modern-day Albany down to the mouth

Catskills vista. *Library of Congress.*

on the southern tip of Manhattan. Trading posts with farmers, craftsmen and laborers (including slaves from Africa) cropped up to feed, clothe and support the burgeoning communities. Small farms became the norm, as America went through the growing pains endemic to the founding of an independent nation and major world power.

Centered as it was between New York and Boston, and on the banks of a mighty river, the Hudson Valley became ground zero for the British defense against the French invasion from Canada during the French and Indian War in the 1750s, not to mention a site for key conflicts during the American Revolution. (Taking control of the river, a source of transportation, food and communication, was a strategic and tactical maneuver both sides of every conflict tried to accomplish.) The raging political conflicts and the reality of seventeenth- and eighteenth-century American storage and transportation capabilities (or lack thereof) made small farms an essential part of the economy. Following the opening of the Erie Canal in 1825, which provided the first transportation system between New York City and the interior of the country, the population of the state surged, and growing needs supported small family farmers in a way that's unimaginable (but should be revisited) today.

The best way to glimpse (and taste) remnants of the European winemaking tradition remade for a new world—and terroir—in America is at the Brotherhood Winery. Brotherhood Winery, in bucolic Washingtonville, was established in 1839 and is the oldest continually operating winery in the country.

Other wineries also harbor secret keys to the past. Benmarl Winery, a thirty-seven-acre estate in Marlboro, harbors the oldest vineyard in America. It also boasts New York Farm Winery license no. 1.

But there was a two-century-plus gap between Henry Hudson's arrival and the firm establishment of those all-important roots, a gap filled with sociopolitical conflict and confusion, false starts and failures on the grape-growing front.

Between Henry Hudson's initial foray into the region in 1609 and the arrival of other Europeans was a brief period when Native Americans were still able to fish in the river, hunt the deer and game along its banks and farm what's known as the three sisters: corn, beans and squash. European settlers started arriving as early as the 1620s, and the land and the people on the land changed quickly. Moving their kith and kin to a strange new land, these pioneers were understandably unwilling to sacrifice their daily tipple, and they started planting vineyards with all of their French winemaking know-how (and fancy European grape varietals).

Western slope of the Shawangunk Mountains. *New York Public Library*.

The European grapes—used to more temperate weather—withered in the decidedly less hospitable climate of the New World. When the Huguenots planted vines on the hills of the Hudson Highlands in Ulster County in 1677, they couldn't conceive of the fact that such a small act would help foster a multibillion-dollar industry that has created hundreds of thousands of jobs, new avenues of scientific inquiry and untold pleasures over the centuries that followed.

The winemaking industry in the Hudson River Valley Region has survived wars, pestilence and Prohibition to become one of the most innovative and versatile wine regions in the world. Here, it's possible to drink one of more than a dozen Gold Medal wines—from brut sparkling to raspberry—at the magical Baldwin Vineyards on the Hardenburgh Estate (circa 1786) and gaze out at thirty-seven acres of prime alluvial farmland or kick back at Adair Vineyards in New Paltz, located in a two-hundred-plus-year-old historic dairy barn with views of the Shawangunk Mountains, and wander the grounds and vineyard with your dog while sipping their Mountain Red, a blend of farm-grown reds.

Dignitaries standing at the dedication of Franklin D. Roosevelt's home at Hyde Park, New York. *Photo by Abbie Rowe; courtesy of the National Archives and Records Administration.*

Mike Melnyk's antique John Deere tractor with fall mums. *Courtesy of FarmOnFoundation.org.*

In the Hudson Valley, more than any other region in the country, winemaking, farm life, sophistication and an unabashed love of all things country are inextricably intertwined.

Throughout the colonial era up to the twentieth century, as vineyards and wineries sprouted, so did sprawling farms. Many of these farms—with stately homes to match—were built by noble American families with familiar bold-faced names like Livingston, Van Cortlandt, Philips, Astor, Van Buren, Rockefeller and Roosevelt.

Many of these homes and the remnants of their farms are still operating in some capacity today and open to the public, including the historic 220-acre Astor property in Columbia County on Empire Road in Copake. Run by the FarmOn! Foundation, the property retains the Empire Farm name, but today it is an educational farm and community center open to the public. It's worth a stroll on the pristine grounds any time of the year, and the doors are always open.

The Philipsburg Manor in Sleepy Hollow is also open to the public, and visitors can see how a typical seventeenth-century farm was managed by the labor of the day (including slaves) and was responsible for growing that food that landed on many people's plates. Check out Appendix E for information on historic Hudson Valley homes open to visitors, many of which also have seasonal farmers' markets and family activities.

In the eighteenth century, about 90 percent of the population in this country were farmers, growing the food and producing drink for the American table. Fast forward to the twenty-first century, and only about 1 percent of the population self-identifies as farmers today.

In the three hundred years that ran between those bookends, the landscape that once provided the breadbasket that supported the American diet—and liquor cabinet—has been developed, razed, built up, torn

Local libations are at the heart of Hudson Valley community. *Courtesy of FarmOnFoundation.org.*

down and disregarded as unproductive rural space that is a drag on the state. Innumerable technological, economic and sociological changes have precipitated this radical shift in the manner in which Hudson Valley residents find employment.

In an effort to revitalize respect for Hudson Valley wine, honor the terroir and simultaneously appreciate the farmers, growers, producers, brewers, distillers and vintners who persevere despite the daunting climactic and geographic challenges without selling out their principles, values or souls to the highest bidder, who remain committed to satisfying our demanding community cravings, it's time to celebrate local libations as we already do local food.

As Hudson Valley Fresh Dairy co-op owner and farmer Jim Davenport said, the land here can be a mother—but not in the *nature* sense. Hudson Valley producers are fighting an uphill battle with nature, starting with unpredictable and severe weather patterns, challenging price competition inflicted by Big Ag and big-box stores in an environment of economic uncertainty. Compound that with pressure from land developers who contributed to making the beloved region the tenth most threatened agricultural area in America with investment interests as far back as 1997, and you will understand what a difference your local spend makes not only for consumption but also for the future preservation of our resource-rich agricultural community.

At the turn of the twenty-first century, farmers, growers and winemakers started taking action to reclaim their fields—and wallets—on their own terms. We have followed their lead, for health and wellness for ourselves and our community and demanding taste worthy of a culinary spend that multiplies to rebuild local economies in rural America.

Locally sourced, honestly made farm-fresh organically grown food and drink has commanded the attention of everyone from the *New York Times* to *Vogue* and Meryl Streep to André Balazs and the pioneering Rockefeller family in the Hudson River Valley region, reinvigorating farming with more respect and revitalizing the region as an economic engine that can and does.

In 2003, the Roundout Valley Growers Association was created to strengthen the health of farm businesses and launch an initiative for healthier school food. That same year, Tuthilltown Spirits founded the state's first legal whiskey distillery since Prohibition. While that may seem only tangentially related to farming, the fact is, distilled spirits can significantly increase the value of fruits or vegetables used in their creation—without sacrificing quality or adding chemicals, additives or preservatives.

Also, in 2005, Glynwood, an educational institution and sustainable farm, launched a much-needed study that finally provided previously scarce data and statistics on Hudson Valley agriculture—making it a local go-to resource for farmers and legislators who wanted to foster economic development and encourage sustainable farming practices to preserve the terroir, the community and commerce. All of this responsible farming leads to the production of enough food and drink—and employment—to nourish our region beyond food, wine, community, character and tourism, by preserving open land, magnificent views and our magical terroir.

According to the most recent report from Glynwood, in 2010, if residents in the Hudson Valley region, combined with New York City's population, spend just 10 percent of their food dollars on regional and locally sourced farm products, that allocation would translate into a whopping $4.5 billion in sales alone.

Agricultural products, whether they are edible or quaffable, are inextricably linked. The relative success of the people who make a living growing, making and selling agriculture has an almost immeasurable effect on the quality of life and economic status of the community in which they are located. Few know

Farmers kick ass. *Courtesy of FarmOnFoundation.org.*

that better than Governor Andrew Cuomo. In 2016, he announced a plan to spend an unprecedented $55 million promoting New York State to draw visitors here. A $2 million slice of that pie was dedicated to promoting agriculture alone.

"As chair of the Regional Economic Development Councils, I have traveled to every corner of the state and have seen first-hand the economic benefits of investing in

Road trip! A map of all the wine regions in New York State. *Courtesy of the Wine and Grape Foundation.*

the tourism industry, which has now become our fourth largest employment sector," Lieutenant Governor Kathy Hochul said when the governor announced the allocation at the New York State Tourism and Craft Beverage Summit in October 2016. "Coupled with that success is the seemingly exponential growth in the number of wineries, breweries, distilleries and cideries, which not only bring jobs and tax revenue but also serve as major tourism drivers. By bringing together tourism, agritourism and craft beverage leaders, we will streamline success and allow these industries to continue to flourish in New York State."

New York gets it. More than any other state, many of which have cut back on tourism spending, New York understands that drawing people to the fields and vineyards of our great state to experience consumption at the source will not only boost the local economy but also give visitors a tangible taste of the rich history and culture the region offers.

The notion that few Michelin-starred restaurants in New York City would deign to have a page devoted to Hudson Valley vintages is slowly changing.

While their menus pen love letters to the region's farmers, distillers and small-batch producers, the grapes of the Hudson Valley were not earning widespread accolades or inspiring an unquenchable thirst in the wine-guzzling populace—until now.

"Restaurants follow critics and consumer demands," said Linda Pierro, co-founder of *Hudson Valley Wine* magazine. "We have found that once people start coming in asking for specific wines, they appear on the wine lists. Chefs and restaurateurs are still often more focused on sourcing local foods over local wines, but that's starting to change as people come in and ask for producers by name."

It's time to get comfortable and connected to our historic home of wine and justify grabbing a bottle of locally produced wine as our first choice. We love our neighbors and our community even more than our tried-and-true Cali pinot, and trying a new sip from the fields can become as eagerly anticipated an event as sampling unfamiliar regional cheeses, a new heirloom tomato or that funky-looking summer sausage calling your name from the farmers' market stall over yonder. The more esoteric the varietal, the more offbeat the hybrid, the more game we are to give it a whirl, or a swirl, as it were.

We've discovered new varietals and hybrids that we didn't know existed—and we love comparing and contrasting Hudson Valley Heritage

Concord grapes hung on a fence. *New York State.*

Taste NY spirits store. *New York State.*

Reds and Whites from winery to winery. We've even abandoned some of our notions about what wine is (it doesn't have to be made from grapes), but most of all, we've gained a new appreciation for getting dirty and the soil under our fingernails as we get deeper into the Hudson Valley terroir and the taste of tomorrow, today.

Along this journey, we've met some of the amazing producers, scientists, sommeliers, innovators, entrepreneurs and elected officials who are making the hills of the Hudson Valley a much livelier and more delicious place to be thanks to vineyards, the farmers and the chefs who are collaborating with the winemakers to create one of the most authentic food and wine scenes in the world as we dare to dream the dream.

"So what can I do?" is the common refrain we hear every day throughout our work building an agricultural community with farmers, winemakers, chefs, legislators, food activists, consumers, peers, family and friends who are trying to promote a more just and sustainable way of life.

The problem of creating a more economically viable and sustainable agricultural system seems so grand, so sprawling, so overwhelming. Don't get it wrong—it is. But the solution is surprisingly simple: meet your farmer, your winemaker, your rancher, your fisherman, your distiller and get connected to what you consume. Not only will they give you something delicious to eat and drink, but also they'll give you insight into the historic roots, planted in the seventeenth century, that we are still harvesting physically, spiritually and intellectually, today.

The American farming family is our link to an edible revolution. Support them every day in every way by eating and drinking local. Make one part of every meal the product of a family farm from down the road. It's the least you can do. Welcome to Hudson Valley wine. Back to the farm we go!

1

TERROIR TELLS THE TRUTH

*E*very parcel of soil on earth tells the story of the region, in the past, right now—and often, it holds the key to its future. The Hudson Valley terroir is pure magic. Celebrated as black gold, the soil is the byproduct of melting glaciers that gave way to the gorgeous Hudson River Valley, and it produces food, wine and other celebrated products of this region.

Terroir, like other borrowed words in English, has absorbed all manners of subjective definitions, like hors d'oeuvres. Literally, terroir comes from the French word *terre*, or land. It encompasses the habitat, elevation, environment, topography and soil of a place. The soil itself is the sum of its historical parts, the result of shifting, evolving land masses and natural disasters. The climate (and the changing climate) affects terroir, as do any adjacent bodies of water, which can provide a mellowing effect to harsh extremes.

Wine is particularly subject to the vagaries of terroir. Wines from a particular region capture flavor from the soil and are incapable of being identically reproduced outside that area, even if the same exact grape varietal and growing methods are used.

C'EST FOU!

Wine is popular, dazzling, mysterious and intimidating, a drinkable metaphor for life itself, embodying joy, possibility, hope and change. Wine remains loyal

Tractor plowing a field at Empire Farm.
Courtesy of FarmOnFoundation.org.

to the land it springs from but owes the pleasure it imparts to the person who takes painstaking care to curate terroir to taste.

The care in the Hudson Valley is almost always mixed with pain.

The Hudson Valley, America's first heartland and the country's birthplace of wine, has—for better and for worse—one of the most diverse terroir landscapes in the Northeast.

The landscapes of the Hudson Valley conjure up a variety of dramatic images, many of which are in violent contrast with one another. Frigid winters, sultry summers, vertiginous cliffs, inviting meadows rolling between the hills, rich soil and gravelly shale-inflected shallow dirt all coexist, but snaking through every image, the river meanders like a mighty but humble god.

The landscape of the Hudson Valley is an instantly recognizable trope in our mind's eye, a symbol of America itself. There's the crystal mountain water sluicing through ancient rock formations created by melting glaciers. Just looking at images of the land, you can almost feel the cold winter winds howling through the hills and valleys, the blazing blasts of July sun searing every blade of grass in its wake and the mighty Hudson River tempering the severity of each extreme with soft river breezes.

And all of this you taste in every glass of wine.

This is terroir.

The Hudson Valley served as the cradle of America's civic life, our explorers, politicians, business tycoons, artists and scientists. As America was formed on paper, the Hudson Valley literally transformed from a sparsely populated patch of inhospitable land into a thriving center of intellect, spiritual discourse, culture and commerce. Fields were tilled, stone walls were erected, homes were planned and history was established as communities began to flourish.

America's thoughts, visions and sounds followed and echoed the Hudson Valley's wide, courageous stride.

Our taste buds followed.

Do you dare enter Brotherhood Winery's historic cellar? *Courtesy of Brotherhood Winery.*

To be fair, chefs "got it" first. Thanks to pioneering talents such as Dan Barber, Mario Batali, David Burke, Terrance Brennan, Zak Pelaccio and Jean-Georges Vongerichten who prize sourcing, technique and polish as much as they do farm-fresh ingredients, the Hudson Valley has been an incubator for the locavore revolution for decades, and local chefs have kept local wineries in business when the public was fickle and obsessed with French wine.

Lydia Higginson, the executive director of Dutch's Spirits and previously the vice president of Dutchess County Tourism, has a unique bird's-eye view of the way restaurant menus and consumer tastes can sometimes dovetail, sometimes lead each other and definitely lift up entire communities with the choices they make.

"Restaurateurs and chefs are so busy," Lydia explains. "They have immense time constraints and are often operating on a razor-thin margin. So when a wine sales rep comes in with a list of six thousand wines, most of them French, often they pick from their portfolio and move on to their next project instead of thinking about the winery twenty-five miles down the road who is producing a fantastic wine at a similar price point."

That's starting to change though. "Farm-to-table was first," she said. "Consumers started demanding local food, and chefs and restaurants followed their lead if they weren't already committed to using products from area farmers." And now, publications like *Modern Farmer*, the *Valley Table* and *Edible: Hudson Valley*, *Edible: Capital District*, *Hudson Valley Wine* magazine and *Columbia Greene Media*'s weekly column "Meet Your Farmer" are educating consumers about the merits of locally produced wines, and they're starting to ask for them by name at restaurants, she explained.

Some restaurants have shown particular leadership in the area and have been offering local wines, beers and spirits for years, including Terrapin, Crave, Artist's Palate and Gigi's, according to Lydia.

Why has it taken so long?

Well, while foodies have been flocking to the hills and hollers of the valley for decades to enjoy our trademark bounty of delectable dairy, astounding apple orchards, creative creameries and grass-fed free-range poultry and beef, the Hudson Valley's wine has been less, shall we say, preferred by our nation's sommeliers, not to mention the average American consumer, unable to decipher points needed to earn prizes and inspire purchase.

Most Americans just don't know (or, until recently, care to know) much about wine. Lack of knowledge leads inevitably to an inability to articulate what they want. Instead of straying outside our comfort zones, it's easier to stick with what we know. In the world of wine, that means California Chardonnays and French everything else.

It's been like that here—everywhere, really—for decades. While Lydia and many others see immense progress in the opening of the American palate, there's still work to be done, so that not only can the basic but deeply rewarding sensual experience of tasting something novel and delicious be indulged but so that our local communities can reap the fiscal and emotional benefits of supporting thriving, small agricultural industries. (You prefer to drive past a bucolic farm or vineyard rather than another sad strip mall, wouldn't you?)

Tessa Edick with Sunday Supper chefs. *Courtesy of Cayla Zahoran Photography.*

We've all read Proust. Well, maybe not. Even if *Remembrance of Things Past* will forever remain a bucket list item on our virtual bookshelf, we're familiar with the infamous Madeleine concept. A bite, a smell or a sip of the flavors reminiscent of your own hearth and home, especially when you're far away, has a powerful, almost mystical, ability to comfort, nourish and reassure. *À la recherche du temps perdu.* (To finding lost time!)

In our current age of hyper, manic globalization, it's possible for almost anyone anywhere to eat virtually the same meal, with the same drink (in the same shirt, watching the same program, listening to the same music). But four hundred years ago, a journey across the ocean to America meant waving farewell to familiar flavors, recipes, food and libations forever—not to mention friends, family and homeland.

It's no wonder that many settlers thought to bring grape stocks to transplant in their new home. Terroir was instinctively understood and cherished by Europeans embarking for life in a strange land, and to this day, it is our most valuable asset in Upstate New York.

Unfortunately, the complexities of agriculture were not quite so easily grasped. So while settlers carted grapevines with them by land and across the sea to America, they failed to cultivate the same kinds of vineyards they left behind—because how do you transport terroir? *L'impossible!*

European settlers who brought vinifera stocks (grape stocks native to the Mediterranean region) with them to Manhattan in the mid-1600s were challenged by this inconvenient truth. In unfamiliar land, dissimilar soil, a different sundial and unpredictable rain patterns, the grape stocks withered, sickened and died. The grapes might have missed their homeland as much as their caretakers (who likely also felt the deficit of *un grand verre* at the end of another arduous day in this challenging land among a melting pot of strangers).

In our age of extremes (is everyone on either a bender or a cleanse at all times?) it's easy to forget how much wine consumption shaped daily life for thousands of years and the synergetic role that food played in this habit, as part of wellness and health to the consumer at that time.

Wine and humanity go way back. The earliest evidence of wine consumption was found in a Neolithic village in the northern Zagros Mountains. (A team from the University of Pennsylvania Museum, led by Patrick McGovern, used infrared spectrometry, liquid chromatography and a wet chemical test to detect calcium salt from tartaric acid, which occurs naturally in large quantities in grapes alone.) The jars filled with this "resinated" wine from the Neolithic home are thought to date as far back as 7000 BCE.

Cold-hardy grapes like these flourish in the Hudson Valley, drawing complexity and depth from the flinty soil and unforgiving winter weather. Reprinted with permission from *Grapes of the Hudson Valley and Other Cool Climate Regions of the United States and Canada* by J. Stephen Casscles. *Courtesy of Flint Mine Press.*

The production of wine, of course, has always required cultivated crops. Some (like McGovern) even believe that the thirst for wine—and intoxication—led to civilization itself.

In McGovern's book *Uncorking the Past: The Quest for Wine, Beer and Other Alcoholic Beverage*, he claims that agriculture, which began about eleven thousand years ago, was the result of humankind's innate desire to unwind at the end of the day with a nice glass of tawny.

"Available evidence suggests that our ancestors in Asia, Mexico, and Africa cultivated wheat, rice, corn, barley, and millet primarily for the purpose of producing alcoholic beverages," McGovern writes.

The altered consciousness produced by wine and its ilk has been linked to religion through the ages. Greeks worshipped Dionysus and Romans followed suit with Bacchus, and the consumption of ritual wine has been a part of Jewish and Christian practice since biblical times. And while Islam nominally forbids the production and consumption of wine today, historically, it was allowed for medicinal and industrial purposes.

Wine has also, for the most part—despite many disapproving and self-serious critics' efforts—always been linked to fun and celebration.

Archaeologists like McGovern say that wine was consumed nine thousand years ago and the cultivation of wild grapevines and the fermentation of

Wine dinner at Holmquest Farm. *Courtesy of FarmOn! Foundation.*

strains of the wild *Vitis vinifera* subspecies *sylvestris* (ancestor to the modern European strain *Vitis vinifera*) was made possible by the development of pottery during the late Neolithic period in 11000 BCE.

Domestication and development of the vineyards, not to mention the technology to produce it, wouldn't come for many thousands of years.

The regal Grand Monarque Hall on Brotherhood Winery's vast and impressive grounds. *Courtesy of Brotherhood Winery.*

The oldest known winery, with a wine press, fermentation vats and storage ephemera, was found in a cave in Armenia, dating to roughly 4100 BCE. Vines and seeds were also found on site. The domestication and consumption of grapes spread quickly through trade, warfare and empire-building. Wine was an essential component of ancient Egyptian life, ancient Greece, ancient China and the Roman Empire.

Throughout history, anthropologists speculate that the large-scale movement of people from country to country, whether due to war, economic opportunity or reasons of religion, included the large-scale movement of seed, horticulture, technology and know-how.

That includes the mass move of immigrants from Europe to America. Today, we are sipping the hard-won fruit of centuries of collaboration between scientists, innovators, farmers and winemakers. Finally, in 2017, the years of failed experiments and withered vines have been transformed. It just took decades of tinkering with hybrids, exacting growing methods, obsessive attention to detail and an understanding, through trial and error, of the manner in which soil, sunlight and seed interact. That hard-won fruit is a pretty sweet sip, especially when enjoyed on one of the many tasting room porches dotting the valley. (Turn to Appendix F for a guide.)

Of course, whether or not the taste for a tipple led to the dawn of civilization is still an item of debate among the scholarly and the barfly set alike, and though we are certainly not seeking to settle it here, feel free to discuss over your next (local) libation.

One thing is clear: in the Hudson Valley, the powerful thirst for a nip of home terroir helped drive European settlers to new heights of ingenuous scientific enterprise and entrepreneurship, the spirit of which is still in practice to this day. (Thirst for wine also sped up the process.)

Homesick Dutch and Huguenot settlers may have planted their grape stocks in the Hudson Valley region in the seventeenth century, but commercial production didn't begin until much later. By the early 1800s, it was clear that European vinifera—or at least the settlers' approach to cultivating it—simply couldn't survive the wild weather fluctuations endemic to the Hudson Valley.

Determined to continue the grand tradition of winemaking in one form or another, the settlers eagerly crushed native grapes and made wine from them. Yet the first vineyard-to-bottle pioneers in America weren't universally thrilled with the results. The wild grapevines colonialists and settlers did find flourishing in the Hudson Valley—*Vitis labrusca*, *riparia* and *vulpina*—did not produce wines that they found palatable. Grabbing wild grapes and pressing them, even if the end product lacked the panache and polish colonialists were seeking, was one thing, but creating and cultivating entire vineyards was another.

In the next chapter, we will explore the paths—sometimes off cliffs, sometimes leading to dead ends and, at other times, to grape nirvana—winemakers, scientists and innovators explored to bring the Hudson Valley wine industry into the modern era, winning prestigious awards and filling crystal goblets in the most rarefied restaurants in Manhattan.

The beginning of that road is too often forgotten. The fact that American winemaking was midwifed in the Hudson Valley is something most of us don't know or have been made to forget. Before California was incorporated as a state, even before Lincoln was president, the wine industry was fermenting in our rich Hudson River Valley cellars, creating history and honing an art. It's tempting to accentuate the bold strides that the Hudson Valley made and attempt to diminish other regions' impressive accomplishments, but that type of back-biting regionalism is short-sighted and part of the reason the American wine industry has struggled to compete on the world stage. We're so busy one-upping each other, we forget to focus on what matters: delicious, responsibly produced

Millbrook Vineyards and Winery booth at Taste NY. *Courtesy of FarmOnFoundation.org.*

wine that works in partnership with the land and the people who care for and consume it.

Until recently, defining what qualifies as delicious and finding the Hudson Valley wines that exemplify it *and* can stand up against an example of the same varietal from California or even the Finger Lakes has been a challenge.

True, taste is subjective. But let's face it: Hudson Valley wines have not historically knocked sommeliers' socks off or won the big awards—until now.

A few highlights:

- Benmarl won a silver for its 2014 Cabernet Franc.
- Glorie Farm Winery also won a silver for the Cab Franc.
- Millbrook Vineyards earned a silver for its 2013 Cabernet Franc Proprietor's Special at the 2016 New York Wine & Food Classic (commonly known as the Oscars of wine competitions).
- Millbrook and Whitecliff also earned ninety points for their Cabernet Francs in the ultra-competitive Wine Enthusiast Competition.
- Baldwin Vineyards earned a gold for its Spiced Apple in the Finger Lakes International Wine Competition.

Made from ripe black currants, cassis is a traditional French liqueur, given a fresh farm-to-bottle twist at the award-winning Brookview Station Winery. *Courtesy of Brookview Station Winery.*

The list goes on. And on. And on. New York wines are winners! That winemakers and locals can finally declare this with confidence (and show the accolades to prove it) has been an almost surreal experience for some in the industry.

"The Hudson Valley has been put on the back burner for so many years, I really can't explain how satisfying it is to see it finally get recognition," Karen Gardy, the director of marketing at Goold Orchards and Brookview Station Winery and the director of the Hudson-Berkshire Beverage Trail, explains. "The Hudson Valley is the crowning jewel of winemaking in America. It started here—we are the oldest winemaking region in the country! And one thing that our region can offer that no one else in the country can is the incredibly diverse offerings. If you go to the Finger Lakes or Napa, all you have is the wineries. They're beautiful. But here, visitors can dig into the country's historical roots and culture—and visit other agricultural producers."

In the Hudson Valley, significant strides in recent decades for production have been made by launching cooperative winemaking organizations and working with scientists at Cornell University to determine the tastiest varietals and hybrids that will flourish here. It happened in perfect tandem with New York State governor Andrew Cuomo's vision and commitment to local producers, culminating in wines are now worthy of your dollars—and homegrown bragging rights.

Critics, many of whom are based in New York, are spreading the word. *Wine Spectator* has rated Millbrook Winery's Chardonnay and Cabernet Franc as good or very good and rated the vineyard itself as one of the best wineries to visit in the area, which passes for delirious adulation in the wine world. Similarly, the magazine bestowed a ninety-six on Baldwin Vineyard's Landot Noir. And yes, celebrated Manhattan chefs who used to say *au revoir* to any wines emerging from New York State are starting to feature some Hudson Valley wines on their menus as a must. *Wine Enthusiast* and the notoriously selective Smorgasburg (a rigorously curated local food and libation festival launched in Brooklyn and now taking place in Kingston, New York, and Los Angeles, California) are eagerly promoting regional wines for the first

Above: Hearty and vigorous, the Baco Noir is a French American hybrid considered by many to flourish with particular aplomb in the Hudson Valley. Reprinted with permission from *Grapes of the Hudson Valley and Other Cool Climate Regions of the United States and Canada* by J. Stephen Casscles. *Courtesy of Flint Mine Press.*

Left: Wine cellars in Pleasant Valley, New York. *Library of Congress.*

time, with Millbrook Winery Chardonnay and Hudson-Chatham Baco Noir getting the love.

The Amorici Vineyard, Bashakill Vineyard, Benmarl Winery and Stoutridge Vineyard brands are getting shout outs from the Smorgasburg crew as destination-worthy vineyards with deliciously drinkable tipples.

By no means are we trying to persuade anyone that the Hudson Valley produces the best wine in the country—yet. The desire to drink homegrown

Storm and Shadow looking over their vast dominion. *Courtesy of the Hudson-Berkshire Beverage Trail.*

grapes goes deeper than that. It's pride of place. It's about the changes that New Yorkers as sustainably minded eaters and drinkers are implementing in their lives. It's about celebrating our home turf, a patch of land where we dwell and hang our hats, and inviting visitors to visit, tour and swing through our history to support the people who are trying to make a go of an art and science as old as dirt, while making a living working the land, celebrating the terroir and contributing to the beauty, culture and economic vitality of their surrounding community.

Instead of reaching for a strawberry in January shipped in from Mexico, most eco-conscious New Yorkers will grab a local apple grown within fifty miles of their home or share the preserves they made from June's strawberries in anticipation of their future craving. Not everything has to be local all of the time (avocados will never grow in Copake, and yet guacamole will always be in our lives), but as our roots get ever deeper in the historic Hudson River Valley and as we continue to build on the idea of locally sourced food having an effect on so much more than just our taste buds, let us consider the excellent effort and opportunity our terroir does offer and our vintners exemplify in producing some excellent bottles worth seeking out for our tables, special occasions and cellars.

The best part? Thanks to an influx of state and private capital investments, environmentally responsible scientific innovations and our savvy New York State governor, the oldest wine scene in the country is finally making the world stage by earning the accolades while remaining true to honest practices in production.

2

MEET YOUR ANCESTRAL WINEMAKER

*I*t's hard to escape the exhortation to "Meet Your Farmer!" these days. It's official: America drank the proverbial farm-to-table Kool-Aid. We continue approving the building of gardens at schools (and visiting the kitchen garden at the White House—thank you, First Lady Michelle Obama, the founder and visionary), running to the farmers' market to buy ugly (but delish) tomatoes and fruit and gossiping about food waste and solutions to food insecurity. We are living this edible revolution, but many in New York still draw the line at our beloved fermented grape juice—Hudson Valley wine. It seems like there's only room for so much edginess in one's diet. Do we really have to start drinking a glass of Baco Noir or Traminette from down the street with a massaged kale salad?

The answer is *yes*. OK, maybe you don't *need* to, but if you value your connection to *your* terroir and want that perfect something to enjoy with your seasonally appropriate farm-fresh meal, your dining experience will be greatly enhanced if you choose a local wine made from grapes that grow well in your soil. The adage *what grows together, goes together*, is certainly true for food and wine pairings. Chef Gianni Scapin in Rhinebeck and the James Beard award–winning chef Zak Pelaccio at Fish & Game in Hudson are maestros at local food and wine pairings. Both restaurants should be stops on any Hudson Valley wine and food adventure.

Any extensive time spent at wineries in the Hudson Valley shows visitors not only how much physical ground there is to cover but also just how diverse that ground is.

The FarmOn! staff love local libations. *Courtesy of FarmOnFoundation.org.*

"There isn't another wine region in America that has so much diversity within its boundaries," Karen Gardy says. "In a matter of fifty miles here you could have a five-degree temperature difference between farms, depending on how close they are to mountains and the river. The microclimates create pockets of incredible diversity, so there is room to explore completely different varietals in lower Hudson Valley, mid Hudson Valley and upper Hudson Valley. The terroir here can be experienced and tasted in radically different forms throughout the valley."

It goes beyond literal taste though, Karen says. "The vibes of Orange, Westchester, Putnam and Dutchess County are all different too. Visitors from within the state and beyond have an incredible opportunity to experience the rich history and layers of stories that have accumulated for four centuries of political and social upheaval here. You just won't find that elsewhere."

(Turn to Appendix F for a few of our favorite mini wine and food itineraries, with restaurants, wineries and historic homes within easy driving distance of one another.)

Thanks to local chefs with cosmopolitan foodways and shows like *Bizarre Foods with Andrew Zimmern* or the ubiquitous Anthony Bourdain, the vast majority of the Gen X and Millennial generation wants to try "crazy" tastes never heard of prior. They (and we) explore the world through our palates, connecting to the stories behind the labels, the makers themselves and the who, what, where, when and why of the crop and the manner in which it was cultivated in the first place. That's mighty convenient in resource-rich regions like the Hudson Valley, with climates that require out-of-the-box farming methods, not to mention some seriously smart hybrid action as boots on the ground.

Some grape varietals that grow well here—many of them, actually are hybrids developed and relentlessly tested by brilliant Cornell University scientists and innovative vintners in New York—as unfamiliar as they are to those of us whose palates were trained sipping the noble varieties, are revelations. (Historically, white noble grape varieties are Sauvignon Blanc, Riesling and Chardonnay; the red noble grapes are Pinot Noir, Cabernet Sauvignon and Merlot.)

Now more than ever, winemakers in the Hudson Valley are discovering the layers of complexity and lip-smacking yumminess that can be teased out of unfamiliar grapes bred to blossom in our region's varying climate and terrain.

It's taken hundreds of years, unrelenting pride, determination and ingenuity to get where we are with Hudson Valley winemakers; finally, our wines are being recognized globally for distinction—and distribution. Without this talent of the winemaker, Hudson Valley wine would remain sweet and unstable, and the industry would be making wine nominally, as a hobby for nostalgic tourists, instead of contributing mightily to the $4.8 billion impact, according to NewYorkWines.org, wine makes on the state's economy.

But before we drill down and meet some of the forefathers of the current Hudson Valley wine movement, we have to pan back. There are a few key landmark events that helped pave the way to our current Renaissance in the history of American wine:

1562: French Huguenots make the first known wines in America from the native Muscadine grape called, inauspiciously, Scuppernong. (The flavor profile leaves, perhaps inevitably, much to be desired.)

1619: After struggling with the taste that native labrusca vine wine produced in Virginia, Lord Delaware attempts to grow European Vitis vinifera *grapes and fails.*

Grapes on the vine. *Courtesy of New York State.*

1650–1700: Franciscan missionaries plant Mission grapes (hailing from Mexico) in Texas, Arizona, New Mexico and California.

1740: John Alexander discovers the first naturally occurring hybrid of vinifera and labrusca grapes near his home in Pennsylvania. Dubbed the Alexander grape, it would be planted in several regions through the early nineteenth century. The fruit fell out of favor for its foxy flavor, but it was a key discovery.

1798: John Dufour launches a commercial winery in Kentucky. The vineyard succumbs to harsh winters and is abandoned just eleven years later.

Duly noted, it is back to the Hudson Valley and the visionaries who, like us, fell in love with the region's temporal extremes and challenges—which less charitable outsiders and observers sometimes characterize as flaws—and saw fit to dig in and plant grapes, naysayers be damned.

The first farmland that would revolutionize winemaking in New York was purchased early on in the nineteenth century. In 1804, Robert A. Underhill bought 250 acres on Croton Point for farming. In 1829, he died, leaving the farmland to his sons, Richard and William. Richard, with 85 acres, planted grapevines imported from Europe with the intention of producing a commercial wine. Underhill purchased the vines from Andre Parmentier, a wealthy Belgian who landed in Brooklyn after fleeing the French Revolution. (William, meanwhile, manufactured bricks on his 165-acre plot.)

The cultivation of these European vines failed (the climate, the land and the soil, as noted previously, were incompatible with the delicate European grapes typically planted), but he spent the next two decades experimenting with grape varieties to figure out what could thrive.

In 1872, he planted native Catawba and Isabellas to start and cultivated them until they took up about seventy-five acres. The grapes were sold in New York City. Underhill planted other native strains, including Delaware and Concord. He also started crossbreeding the native and European vines until he established hardy species that could flourish in the Hudson Valley and exude the refinement and complexity of flavor so beloved in the European strain.

These grapes were true New Yorkers: sophisticated, chic survivors.

One of the hybrids was named Croton, a cross between Delaware and Chasselas de Fontainbleau, and another was Senasqua, a cross between Concord and Black Prince, aka Cinsaut. The Underhills started commercially selling their wine in 1859 and began garnering awards for the products themselves and for the genius behind the hybridizations, Richard Underhill.

But before Richard Underhill began cultivating his first vines, the French Huguenot Jean (John) Jacques began setting the stage to launch what has become the oldest operating winery in America: the Brotherhood Winery.

Many winemakers in the Hudson Valley literally open the doors of their homes for visitors who want to sample their creations. *Courtesy of the Hudson-Berkshire Beverage Trail.*

In 1810, Jacques purchased farmland in the Hudson Valley and began planting and cultivating native Isabella and Catawba grapes. By 1837, he had decided to buy more land, this time purchasing a plot in Washingtonville and planting another vineyard. He dug underground cellars, purchased the most modern winemaking equipment available (including corking machines and fermenting casks) and produced his first commercial vintage in 1839. It was sold under the label Blooming Grove Winery.

That winery, established in 1839, is America's earliest continually operating winemaker and possibly its most intriguing. It has continuously adapted is modus operandi to the changing political and sociological mood of the country and, perhaps more importantly, its ever-shifting palate over its 175-year history.

For two decades, the Jacques family produced wines under the Blooming Grove label for commercial and religious purposes; when Jean passed away in 1858, his three sons renamed the winery Jacques Brothers' Winery.

Meanwhile, just across the river, a rather, ahem, unique (read: cult-like) community led by Thomas Lake Harris (1823–1906) that called itself the Brotherhood of New Life founded its own winery. Sound creepy? Just wait.

Between 1860 and 1864, the community produced wine that it believed was suffused with divine power. (Harris also claimed that God was bisexual, advocated the use of tobacco and demanded complete devotion from his followers, who eventually numbered two thousand.) While few outside of their commune were thirsty for their spiritual succor, they certainly guzzled down Harris's wine. The wine found drinkers throughout the United States and even in Europe and Africa. In 1865, the commune moved to Lake Erie, and father-and-son wine merchants in New York City, Jesse and Edward Emerson, purchased Harris's winery. Esoteric spirituality was on the out list, a newfound infusion of vinicultural expertise in.

In 1866, the Emersons bought the Blooming Grove Winery from Charles Jacques, the last living Jacques brother, and merged the two. The Emersons, former publishing moguls, knew a good story when they saw it and decided to capitalize on the racy Brotherhood name and reputation, while using the modern Washingtonville facility and well-placed vineyard to grow and produce the wine.

They were the first of many larger-than-life guerrilla Hudson Valley wine marketers. Brotherhood Winery has changed hands a number of times, but despite significant setbacks and challenges, it has managed to navigate 176 years of economic strife, Prohibition (the winery remained operational by providing wine for religious services), wars and changing palates by always staying a few steps ahead of the market.

Not every vintner at Brotherhood has won top marks for the quality of their wine (many of their products do or could fall into the less, shall we say, appreciated dessert wine category), but every single one has been a marketing genius. Visit the vineyard yourself (see our guides in the appendices) and see why it's so successful. (Spoiler alert: it's stunningly

Pen and ink sketch of GM Hall. *Courtesy of Brotherhood Winery.*

gorgeous and probably the best example of what people expect a vineyard to look like from the movies in the Hudson Valley.)

Andrew Jackson Caywood, a young farmer who bought a patch of land overlooking the Hudson River in Marlboro in the early 1800s, was another hardworking pioneer who helped clear a path in the rocky Hudson Valley soil. That particular region had been growing grapes since 1772, and when it was incorporated as the Village of Marlborough in 1788, the powers that be selected a cluster of grapes as its symbol. Caywood became one of the foremost grape tinkerers of his time. He successfully crossbred vinifera and native grapes, developing strains like the Dutchess, which is still grown here today.

By the time Mark Miller bought the land, it had outlived all of its contemporaneous vineyards to inherit the mantle as America's oldest professional vineyard.

Miller (d. 2008), another publishing guru turned vintner, bought that storied crop of land in 1957 and, like the Emersons before him, cannily capitalized on and disseminated the history and story of the land while improving the wine it produced. Miller was hardly the first modern winemaker in the valley, but he was absolutely the most audacious and omniscient. From the get-go, Miller pushed the limits of even the hippiest-dippiest of eras and regions as a relentless advocate of artisanal winemaking.

Unlike his contemporaries, he spurned grapes that produced sweet, bombastic, obvious one-note wonder champagnes and ports. He ignored critics and scientists who said the soil was too rocky and the climate too extreme to cultivate subtle, sophisticated flavors.

He named the forty-acre vineyard Benmarl, allegedly for the Gaelic word *ben*, which means "mountain," and *marl*, for its challenging soil. He rebuilt the vineyard's steep terraces, replanted them with European wine grapes and hybrids and continued to experiment with grape crossbreeding in an effort to tease out the best combination of exuberant hardiness and complex character.

Miller didn't start working the fields in earnest until 1967, after several years studying winemaking in Burgundy. His trademark was using hybrid grapes, which in conservative 1970s wine circles was considered risqué, if not downright tacky. But he persisted, confident that he could produce wines that tasted like France but had the Yankee can-do spirit to withstand the fiercest winter howl and the most wretchedly scorching August sun.

His first commercial bottling happened in 1972, and initially, it was sold for about three dollars a bottle. Less than two decades later, the vineyard

Named after a famous French general from World War I, the Foch grape has also proven to be a brilliant battler against the Hudson Valley climate, flourishing where others fail and wither. *Courtesy of the Hudson-Berkshire Beverage Trail.*

expanded to encompass seventy acres and produce ten thousand cases per year. The grapes it became most known for were Seyval Blanc, Vignoles and Verdelet for white wines, Chelois, Baco Noir and Foch for reds.

In his quest to push the grape to its skin-bursting limits in the Hudson Valley, Miller became a cultural and legislative force. To fund his experimentation, he founded the Societe des Vignerons in the 1970s, essentially a CSA for wines. It allowed investors to buy the rights to two or more of his vines, entitling them to a case of wine a year.

It was a carefree, fun-loving gesture that captured the imagination and hearts of wine lovers and—this is key—helped them invest financially, emotionally and intellectually in regional wine. The program quickly grew from a handful to include hundreds of so-called investors.

For the first time ever, prominent restaurants in New York City were carrying Hudson Valley wines, including Windows on the World, the Four Seasons and the Quilted Giraffe.

Other vintners took notice, and the movement toward accolade-earning splashy *Wine Spectator* profiles began in earnest. Miller was the first winemaker in the Hudson Valley that sommeliers, critics and wine aficionados took seriously.

The Societe—and Miller—was also instrumental in the passing of the first major piece of legislation since the repeal of Prohibition that would support and help New York wineries to earn.

A member of Miller's Societe, New York governor Hugh Carey, signed the Farm Winery Act in 1976. The act allows grape farmers to produce and sell wines directly to the public. Benmarl was awarded New York State Farm Winery License no. 1.

So how can it be that New York, with such a rich history of winemaking and with a grape crop valued at more than $50 million, behind only California and Washington in terms of production, has such a pathetic rep among the nation's wine experts?

For starters, there's the actual taste of New York's native grapes, which, until Miller stepped in, flourished so abundantly in vineyards here. *Vitis labrusca* produce a distinct muskiness (the compound responsible for the aroma has been identified by scientists as methyl anthranilate) commonly characterized in wine-speak as *foxy*. Definitely not a compliment.

Vitis vinifera accounts for less than 10 percent of wine produced in the state in general—and even less in the Hudson Valley specifically—because many of those grapes simply can't hack it here.

Thanks to the visionaries we just discussed and the tireless work of scientists at Cornell University, a wealth of American hybrid grapes, including Catawba, Delaware, Niagara, Elvira, Ives and Isabella, flourish. Yes, the most delicate European grapes can also grow here, but with the Hudson Valley climate, seasonality and ultimately unique terroir, they simply don't thrive as well as they do in Europe or out west of the Hudson Valley.

There is also the all important convenience factor. We live in a world where we can order meals, dates, transportation and all manners of goods with the click of a button. We are accustomed to receiving and being transported to the object of our current whimsical desire almost immediately.

In California, and even regions of Long Island and the Finger Lakes, wineries are clustered in certain areas, so it's a snap to get from one to the other. In the Hudson Valley, they are literally all over the map, and hitting even a handful of wineries would require a day in the car, with a map and patience.

Sometimes, though, the notion of being patient and driving (while carefully monitoring our wine consumption), much less picking which wineries and historical hot spots to hit, is enough to drive any of us to, well, just stay home and drink. There are numerous resources (turn to the appendices for details) for folks who want someone to curate a package for them. Wineries are even embracing the tour bus concept, which, in addition to making great wine, is essential to their viability.

Couple looking at Core vodka. *Courtesy of FarmOnFoundation.org.*

"I used to see resistance to the tour bus thing at wineries, because it's a lot of work," Lydia Higginson, who ran many a tour group all over the county when she was vice president of Dutchess County Tourism, said. "But if the industry is going to thrive, producers are starting to understand that they have to educate consumers, talk to them one-on-one, make them see on a personal level how precious the treasure of open space, diverse terroir and history is here in the Hudson Valley. That's what leads them to ask for a Millbrook or a Whitecliff the next time they're out at dinner. That's what creates real change."

What's holding us back is that we allowed California, through movies, television shows and cultural hegemony, to define the American wine experience. Guess what? There will never be a Hudson Valley version of the infamous winery flick *Sideways*. Like the slow but steady relinquishment of the insistence for noble grape varieties, visitors and tourists—but more essentially, the wineries themselves—have to start thinking about the glorious, unique offerings the Hudson Valley has and position themselves accordingly.

To get to the next level, the Hudson Valley wine industry is starting to align itself with the equally powerful, definitely more adult, cultural zeitgeist that is carving out a more Zen-Buddhist approach to consumerism à la slow food.

One organization leading the way in that regard is the *Valley Table*, a magazine that celebrates the people behind the food and drink made here.

"For Hudson Valley Restaurant Week, the *Valley Table* created a program where they made special cocktails and had special local wines poured at restaurants who were participating," Lydia said. "Not only did it give the public an opportunity to try the wines, it gave the chefs an opportunity to establish a relationship with the winemakers and possibly open up a new avenue of revenue for everyone."

Taste NY is probably the biggest driver of commerce and change, according to Lydia. Taste NY was created in 2013 by Governor Cuomo and his team to promote New York's food and beverages. Overseen by the Department of Agriculture, it was designed to give producers a chance to have the public taste their goods at tourism fairs, state fairs, Thruway stops and in any and all major transportation hubs.

"Taste NY has branded the area in a whole new way," Lydia said. "I credit Andrew Cuomo with understanding the impact tourism has on our state. While other states cut back, New York has embraced the opportunity and has successfully marketed us to the world, aggressively representing us at trade missions. Now, we're reaping the benefits. We have busloads of tourists visiting our vineyards, breweries and distilleries from China, London, all around the world."

Tasting rooms are thinking outside of the wineglass. Many are starting to welcome visitors with cheese pairings (this is dairy country after all, and

Taste NY Spirits Store. *New York State.*

Add local Hudson Valley spirits to Arrowhead Farms mixers. *Courtesy of CulinaryPartnership.com.*

we have some of the best cheese makers in the world right here), chocolate pairings and experiential events.

Instead of hopping from winery to winery, going to visit one and staying for some brick-oven pizza, live music and a personal tour of the natural wine-aging cave or geothermal bottling room has become the norm.

Then there are the laws. New York is an extremely litigious place with enough red tape to choke a vineyard before it has a chance to blossom. Miller, the wine farm act of 1976 and motivated winemakers who have the background and constitution to needle Albany tirelessly have opened New York State up and brought in a whole host of new winemakers. (In 1976, there were just nineteen wineries in New York; now there are more than four hundred.) But Governor Andrew Cuomo has, arguably, done more than any scientist or winemaker in revolutionizing the industry, at last count attracting more than 5.3 million tourists to New York State and supporting twenty-five thousand full-time jobs with wages totaling more than $1.4 billion, which then gets reinvested into the local economy, boosting property values, small businesses and the quality of life up and down the Hudson Valley.

Without the effort of literally centuries of grape growers, scientists, wine entrepreneurs and quite frankly (especially of late) decidedly unglamorous bureaucrats, the vast majority of Hudson Valley wine would still be headed for the liquor store bargain bin.

Hudson Valley wines—for the first time since 1839—are critically acclaimed. A few more crucial love notes: *Wine Enthusiast* gave scores of ninety to Benmarl 2012 Cabernet Franc (Ridge Road, Estate) and Whitecliff 2012 Gamay Noir Reserve. Warwick Valley was rated No. 2 and Red Hook was rated No. 3 in msn.com's 101 Best Wineries in America, and New York State overall was named Wine Region of the Year by *Wine Enthusiast* magazine, citing the tremendous growth of the industry.

"It's the 'thirty-year overnight success,'" Jim Trezise, president of the New York Wine and Grape Foundation, quipped. "The quality of the wines is now world-class, thanks to research at Cornell and collaboration among grape growers and winemakers. The business climate is better than it has ever been for wine."

3

MEET YOUR VINTNER

*L*ocation, by definition, can make or break the success of a destination. How many gourmet restaurants could succeed in a strip mall? Part of the magic of truly elevated cuisine—and the reason we are willing to shell out a partial mortgage payment on special occasions to pay for the privilege—is the setting, the space itself and the patch of land it is parked on.

The best thing going for Hudson Valley wineries, aside from the product itself, is the location.

For the first time, wineries are becoming destinations for wine aficionados, based on their own merit and the blitz of great PR they've received. But for decades, Hudson Valley wineries were loved primarily because they happen to be in the Hudson Valley—a stunning agricultural community, outdoorsy hiking mecca, valley of the light uniquely positioned between Connecticut and New York City, not to mention artisanal in every way with an epicenter of energy ignited by every creative force it encapsulates.

Think of Applewood Winery in Warwick. Located on a forty-acre apple orchard and farm dating back to 1700, it epitomizes Hudson Valley farm chic. Seventeen wines, including everyone's favorite hybrid Traminette as well as old faves like Chardonnay and Cab Franc, are available, along with four varieties of their award-winning apple cider, Naked Flock. Weekends here buzz with concerts on Saturdays and mimosa brunches on Sundays.

Consider Clinton Vineyards in Clinton Corners. With forty years of winemaking experience under its barrel, visitors could be forgiven for thinking they stumbled into France. Between the landscaped grounds,

Farmland in the Taconic Range. *Library of Congress.*

the Dutch barn and the award-winning Seyval Blanc and delicious cassis, an afternoon here definitely feels more like an afternoon in Europe than New York.

More of a slow foodie? Hit up critical darling Hudson-Chatham Winery in Ghent, where wine is painstakingly produced by hand on a one-hundred-year-old-press. Au natural, baby. The tasting room features noshes to match: think artisanal cheese, honey, jam. *Wine Spectator* and *Wine Enthusiast* have both given their austere, much-desired stamp of approval.

Each winery has its charms and its roster of events that reflect its ethos—refined cheese pairings for some, down and dirty grape stomping for others. We love it all.

But now, wineries in the Hudson Valley are finally becoming just as beloved for the hybrid wines they produce too. In many ways, it's a lot easier for winemakers to enchant tourists, critics and restaurateurs when they have a pairing. A glass of skin-fermented Chardonnay in front of you, along with a slice of raw cow or goat's milk cheese sourced from the artisanal cheese maker from down the road and his grass-fed free-range livestock, is enticing all around and heightens the experience.

Ready to hit the fields. *Courtesy of the Hudson-Berkshire Beverage Trail.*

Then pair that moment with a story to savor, while taking in a panoramic view of the Catskills or the Shawangunk cliffs from the comfort of a cozy tasting room lit by fire from locally felled trees and fueled by the energy of city folk who frequent the wineries to frolic in the vineyards and discuss perceptible tannic structures, hints of berries, honey, salinic minerality and the sweetness of the mellow May sunlight.

Visually, the Hudson Valley is inarguably tough to beat for visitors. But for winemakers who live, work and make here, logistically, the demanding terroir can take its toll.

Hudson Valley wineries are spread across a vast geographic region that is inhospitable to most grapes that are widely accepted by the drinking public as delicious. Adding insult to injury, the patches of land available to most winemakers for decent vineyards here are tiny in comparison to other wine regions the world over. That means simple geography makes it impossible for winemakers to scale up, even if they want to, so an immense amount of effort fighting the elements will have to be poured into relatively small vineyards. Bottom line: clearly it is tough to make an honest buck in winemaking in the Hudson Valley. The folks who do persevere and succeed on any scale do so because they love the process, the hard work and the accomplishment so well deserved.

New York is known as the Big Apple and not the Big Grape—for good reason. The variable conditions, the humidity and temperature fluctuations that create hardy, delicious apples wreak havoc on delicate grapes, Chris Gerling, a Cornell University enologist, explained. "There are a lot of challenges in the Hudson Valley for growing grapes," Dr. Gerling, an extension associate at the New York State Agricultural Experiment Station in Geneva, said. "The humidity and the variable temperature, with late freezes in the spring and early freezes in the fall, cause problems when grape buds are ready to blossom or go into dormancy. Frost can wipe out their initial blooms. But some grapes here are doing great. Cabernet Franc, for example, was adopted in the Finger Lakes more than ten years ago, but it has taken to the Hudson Valley much better. Here it's rounder and there's more depth of character. So much depends on the vineyard and its location."

According to Dr. Gerling, much depends on the grower also. "Millbrook has done some incredible work with their Riesling and the experiments they are willing to commit to with new varieties and hybrids," he said. "The goal when growing should always be to have a wine with characteristics that meet or exceed what is currently available, but with better disease resistance and hardiness. If you'll only plant vinifera, you'll have to spray a lot more. But if you plant hybrids specifically developed for the region, like Traminette, which mimics the more familiar Gewürztraminer in taste, but doesn't require as much spray, you're going to have a much healthier grape."

Not to mention a glass of wine sans a pesticide spritzer, a healthier landscape and a happier grower who doesn't need to spend all of his or her time in the field obsessing over a delicate bunch of grapes.

But the challenges don't stop with the weather.

Trevor Valley Farm Riesling grapes at press. *Courtesy of Michael Rietbrock and Susan Pearson.*

The dramatic landscape—sudden peaks and valleys, fewer naturally graded hills and gradual elevations—that creates such visual interest also causes more planting and harvesting demands than most winemakers ideally want to contend with.

On what many speculate is a related note, the words *colorful* and *tenacious* are frequently deployed by the more tactful members of the Hudson Valley wine community when describing the winemakers themselves. Those who choose to forgo subtlety and politesse often deploy phrases like "stubborn as hell" and "intense" when discussing Hudson Valley winemakers. But even the barbs are shared with an overwhelming sense of admiration for these pioneers who do battle with the climate, landscape and visitors who demand drive-through convenience in the sprawl of a countryside that constitutes Hudson Valley wine world. Perhaps in addition to particular plants, it takes a particular personality profile to perfect preservation of viticulture in the Hudson Valley.

It isn't a far stretch to liken the tough winemakers to the tough grapes that manage to flourish. While neither the folks who grow these grapes nor the grapes themselves will ever be accused of diaphanous refinement—and may never be suited for middle-of-the-road mainstream taste—they are distinctive and beloved by those who know and care for them like extended family.

Some of these talented winemakers are so uniquely suited to the mercurial climate, soil and moods of the Hudson Valley that they cannot confine their touch to just one vineyard. Kristop Brown, a relative whippersnapper (at forty-one), has managed to garner the respect and trust commonly earned by folks twice his age. And his résumé is stacked: Kristop started at Millbrook Vineyards, one of the most lauded wineries in the valley, getting his feet wet in the tasting room when he was about twenty-seven.

"Before that, I was living in Montana, and I knew I wanted to get into the wine industry here, so I took a job as a tasting room manager," Kristop recalled. "I ended up helping the winemaker John Graziano. I did everything from washing barrels and scrubbing tanks, in addition to learning the basics of winemaking from him."

Brown loved the camaraderie and sense of adventure inherent in winemaking and seemed to thrive in an atmosphere in which there was always something new to learn and try. He also studied chemistry and biology as an undergrad at Rutgers University, which gives him a huge leg up in a climactically challenging winemaking region that requires absolute precision and a rigorous exactitude to coax beautiful tasting notes from weather-beaten grapes.

"I saw an ad for an assistant winemaking position at Benmarl, and the winery is so legendary, I wasn't confident I'd get it," Brown recalls. "But we hit it off, and they gave me a huge opportunity. I worked under Eric Miller, whose family has been making what many thought to be the best wine in the valley for decades."

After a five-year stint at Benmarl and a trip out west to work at Long Shadows Winery in Washington, Brown was ready to return to the Hudson Valley in 2011. The community welcomed him with open arms, and now he is a free agent, making innovative, gutsy wines at Glorie Farm Winery, Robibero Winery and Clinton Vineyards. (He has also launched a craft brewery, Yard Owl Craft.)

The wineries give Brown full rein, and he takes full advantage, experimenting with obscure clones like the Arctic Riesling at Robibero, which resulted in a fabulously dry wine that is aged in oak for a year and has drawn a cult following for its notes of tropical fruit that balance its dryness.

"My creative process is driven by taste, aroma and experience," Kristop asserted. "I monitor the wines through every step of the process. I crunch numbers and think about the implications. I taste the wine as it is fermenting and a vision of what it will be later emerges. Everything is sensory driven, but the science has to be there too."

Interestingly, his reason for returning to the Hudson Valley is right in line with the increasingly common perception among serious, cutting-edge critics and foodies: "It's just earthier here, it's real. The flavors aren't as clean and simple. They're funky. I've never found a more exciting, diverse region where the terroir can absolutely be tasted."

Digging Terroir at Stoutridge Vineyards

Funk and terroir are the raison d'être at Stoutridge Vineyards, where the founders have launched a unique, counterintuitive project that, even the owners admit, totally should have failed. Epically.

"We couldn't find a bank today who would underwrite what we're doing here," Stephen Osborn, the co-founder at Stoutridge, said, laughing. "In 2005, we hit the sweet spot when eating and drinking local was just getting big and the economy humming along. A bank took a chance on our crazy plan to build a natural winery designed to accurately capture wine, and the terroir of Marlboro, in its purest form."

The wine made at Stoutridge is done completely naturally, which in this case means there is absolutely nothing added. (Like natural food, natural wine isn't defined by an official government entity, and there is some disagreement about what constitutes a natural wine.) Stoutridge is pretty orthodox: no fining, sulfites, pumping, filtering. Absolutely nothing but grapes and gravity.

"Kim [Wagner] and I are both biochemists and winemakers, and we are really interested in how terroir can be truly captured in its purest form by not using extraneous products," Stephen said. Not everyone loves the manner in which natural wine reveals the strengths and challenges of the minerally, what he calls *nervy*, gravelly terroir of the Hudson Valley in an unfiltered way, he admitted. It's like catching a glimpse of a Hollywood beauty without her makeup on—for some, there's nothing more enchanting. Others prefer her with her nose powdered, thanks. There's room for everyone here, according to Stephen: "The thing I love most about winemaking in the Hudson Valley, and I've done it many places, is that literally everyone has a different take on the terroir. A different way to grapple with it. Different grapes they like to plant. It's about nuance. There's room for everyone, as long as they have a vision, and aren't afraid to work twelve hours a day, seven days a week, all in the name of wine."

Talented winemakers like Kristop and Stephen are able, in their insatiable quest for funk and nuanced terroir, to grapple with the ravaging effects of the weather through fearless experimentation balanced by a tirelessly scientific approach to grape-growing and winemaking, pretty much anywhere in the Hudson Valley.

4

DESTINATION HUDSON VALLEY

*N*o matter how many TED podcasts we tune into about the earth, the climate and the nature of nature (Louie Schwartzberg's "Nature. Beauty. Gratitude" and John Doerr's "Salvation and Profit in Greentech" are two favorites), sometimes it's tiresome to spend time wrapping our minds around the broader implications of how piles of rock dust give Hudson Valley wine its signature flair.

So, for those of us without a graduate degree in agronomy, the Hudson Valley crosses five of the nine New York physiographic provinces and has more soil types than any other area of the state. There's the hilly region of the Tolkien-sounding Gneissic Highland Province, also known as southern Rockland County. The hardy bedrock underpinning Westchester, Putnam and southern Dutchess Counties resulted in shallow soils, unsuitable for large swaths of grapes. But in the Taconic Province, extending from Orange through southern Ulster and across the river to northeastern Dutchess, Columbia, Washington and Rensselaer Counties, the shale, slate, schists and limestone rocks, sprinkled with quartzite and gneiss, impart minerality and body to grapes and to fruit in general.

And grapes are finicky.

There are moisture issues and terrain challenges in certain areas, but all of Columbia and much of eastern Dutchess are considered prime grape-stompin' grounds. The mellowing climactic effect of the Hudson River and the fine drainage more than make up for the wrench the steep ridges of the Shawangunk Mountains and the Catskills throw into the works.

In fact, the hills even help us get tastier results. The huge tracts of fertile, flat land used to grow grapes in some blockbuster wine regions (like certain areas of Australia, think Yellow Tail) produce acre-by-acre huge quantities of grapes that can be mechanically harvested. Cheaply produced, they're a dream for canny farmers who are focused only on the bottom line. But wine produced with the same methodology (high yield, cheaply produced) and goals (maximum profit) that big food uses to crank out meat nuggets and gives us asparagus in New York in January has many of the same issues (blah taste, with a side of pesticide).

Dr. Chris Gerling, our go-to wine expert at Cornell University, explains how wine grown on the slopes Hudson Valley winemakers have targeted is so much better than wine grown on flat land.

"The Hudson Valley is actually similar in terrain to Burgundy," Gerling said. "Hillsides in general are much better for vines than flat terrain because on a slope, the grapes receive more sun, with the rays falling at an angle that's perpendicular. On flat land, the sun is more diluted. Slopes also provide more drainage and aeration since the water trickles to the bottom of the slope. In flat areas, the vines can just sit in soil that's too moist."

And then there's the climate.

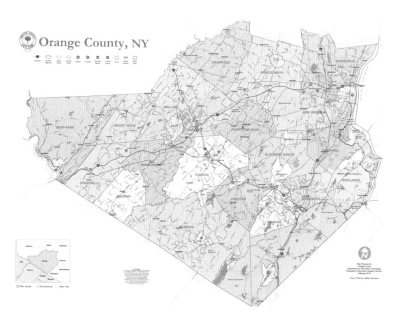

Orange County is beloved for its open land, vineyards and up-and-coming foodie scene. *Courtesy of Orange County Tourism.*

Like Burgundy, the summers here are marked by high heat and humidity, and winters are all over the barometer, with an average of twenty degrees Fahrenheit, but as anyone who lived through 2014–15 can attest, weeks-long blasts of below zero are hardly unheard of. All of this wreaks havoc on grapes, not to mention the droves of birds that feed and decimate the crop even when perfection from nature delivers. And even then, if grapes survive the bipolar extremes of mother nature, the productivity and overall quality can plummet. Also, the lower Hudson Valley (Westchester) and the mid-to-upper Hudson Valley are in two separate macro-climates: the Mid-Atlantic and the New England, respectively.

They have different patterns of temperature, solar radiation and rainfall that all greatly affect grape-growing. The Mid-Atlantic region is moderated by the Atlantic Ocean, which makes the winter milder and autumn longer. The New England region is more extreme, leading to more variable freezes in spring and fall.

Microclimates can be considered in perplexing detail, at the scale of a few centimeters or a portion of a vine, if you really want to geek out and go nuts. Which, if you're serious about producing great wines, you should do. One of the pet peeves of Michael Migliore, the wildly successful (for the Hudson Valley at least) grape-grower and industry brainiac, is a failure to respect the basic tenets of science.

"I have temperature monitors all over the valley," he said. "About 130. Some viniferas are more hardy than others, and a difference of a few degrees can greatly affect the overall taste. Winemakers should also follow best practices, including measuring the acidity and sugar levels of wine as it ferments and studying its malolactic fermentation."

Migliore founded the Whitecliff Winery with his wife, Yancey Stanforth-Migliore, thirty years ago in an empty field in Gardiner. Michael has a background in organic chemistry and engineering, and he puts his science smarts to work every day as a winemaker. Together, they grew the artisanal wine company into a world-renowned operation; their wine is sold in top-flight restaurants like the Gramercy Tavern. Michael is president of the Hudson Valley Wine & Grape Association, and he won the New York State Grower of the Year Award in 2015.

Anyone from a big family knows how bloodthirsty and irrational the competition to be first in something—anything—can be. Advocates for Hudson Valley wine country, perhaps due to its relatively low status in the wine world pecking order, can often be heard crowing about the illustrious firsts the Hudson Valley wine industry can wear on its lapel. Oldest vineyard in America! (Benmarl.) Oldest continually operating winery! (Brotherhood.) There's another—and bonus, it's connected to one of the aforementioned firsts—first center for wine tourism! We are the original Napa of the East.

The Hudson Valley arguably created—and then the West Coast appropriated, in many ways improved upon and certainly capitalized on more successfully—wine tourism.

It's hard to imagine that the wine industry could support so many American wineries—some of which only produce a few dozen cases per year—without the hordes of tourists as eager to soak up local history and legend as they are to swill the local vintage heading to wineries. As of 2016, there were about 8,702 wineries in America according to *Wine Business Monthly*, a 5 percent increase since 2015. The U.S. wine, grape and grape products industries pour more than $162 billion annually into the American economy, a study from MKF Research LLC of Napa Valley found.

In the Hudson Valley wine "dark age" of the 1960s, Brotherhood Winery was struggling to keep up with the West Coast Joneses of Mondavi, Schoonmaker and Gallo and their awarded wines. According to Robert Bedford (publisher of *Hudson Valley Wine* magazine and author of the informative, fascinating biography of the Brotherhood Winery, *The Story of Brotherhood, America's Oldest Winery*), then owners Frances and Eloise Farrel and their daughter Anne essentially created wine tourism to boost sales.

The Farrels had given the winery a much-needed facelift after more than one hundred years of operation, modernizing equipment, renovating buildings and generally making a visit to the winery a more aesthetically engaging and sensory experience. Instead of just forking over a glass of fermented grape juice, the Farrels started giving tours of the winery to visitors, talking about the history of the winery and explaining some of the fine points of tasting and enjoying their wines on the property.

They put thinking and intellectualizing terroir in terms of wine in a safely American context that was part historical, part scientific and, dare we say, fun—stripping away some of the perceived European frippery that has always surrounded wine culture by connecting people to the source, the land and the maker.

The Brotherhood Winery is on the Shawangunk Wine Trail, and like all trails in the Hudson Valley, it is best to approach a visit to the trail as a curated experience that you map out, not necessarily according to geography and palate but also by your goals for understanding the region, its products, people, culture, history—not just the physical properties of the Hudson Valley terroir but also its philosophical and existential offerings.

From the Shawangunk Mountains, painting by Sanford Robinson Gifford of the Hudson River School. *Wikimedia Commons*.

The Shawangunk Wine Trail, sixty miles north of New York City, has something for everyone. The location, between the Shawangunk Mountains and the Hudson River in Ulster and Orange Counties, meanders along for eighty miles and features fifteen wineries that produce anywhere from fewer than two thousand cases a year to upward of fifty thousand.

While the legendary trail is as established in the old winery firmament society as Babe Paley is on Fifth Avenue, there's no need to pack your ascot when hitting the trail. While you will find quiet vistas of mountains, rolling hills and acres of well-staked vineyards at the likes of both Benmarl and Brotherhood Wineries, accompanied by tours of their cellars and tastes of rare vintages, you'll also find decidedly recherché wineries like Robibero, which proudly holds a rousing "green wine" fest on St. Patrick's Day.

Every winery in the Hudson Valley has a different vibe and spin on their fruit juice. And because the wineries aren't nearby to one another, it makes more sense to pick one or two destinations for the day and really immerse yourself in the culture, the land and the spirit of the place to get on the celebration train of our East Coast gems invested in wine production in memorable places.

Revisit the options on a drive through the Hudson Valley with our quick cheat sheet:

WINERIES ON THE SHAWANGUNK TRAIL

Adair Vineyards

CLAIM TO FAME: Farmhouse chic.
NOTES: The winery was established in 1985, cranks out roughly thirty thousand bottles a year and is housed in a picture-perfect red barn. Its wine label features a painting of a solitary oak tree in an appropriately bucolic setting circa 1840 from Hudson River Valley School artist Asher Durand.
PRODUCTION HIGHLIGHTS: Estate-grown and bottled grapes supplemented from local grape grower.

Applewood Winery

CLAIM TO FAME: Small-batch bona fides.
NOTES: Housed on the oldest working farm in Orange County with more than four centuries of continuous operation under its belt, the wine line was launched in 1993 to produce lines of vinifera grape–based wines, apple wines and an increasingly popular hard cider.
PRODUCTION HIGHLIGHTS: Every wine is a limited edition small batch, sold only on site.

Baldwin Vineyards

CLAIM TO FAME: Offbeat, fruity fun.
NOTES: This winery has been unabashedly marching to its own drumbeat for twenty-seven years, producing consistently delicious, unexpected wines and serving them to what always seems to be a convivial, crowded house. Look out for their Chili Fest in June and Strawberry, Chocolate and Wine Festival Weekends in the fall.
PRODUCTION HIGHLIGHTS: The winery is especially beloved for its strawberry wine, especially when paired with cheesecake or chocolate and sipped at the winery, located on the old Hardenburgh Estate from 1786.

Benmarl Winery

CLAIM TO FAME: The real deal.

NOTES: With New York Farm Winery license number one, Benmarl proudly led the way in the Hudson Valley toward estate-grown grapes that can compete on the world stage. Like many wineries here, it is a family affair. Visitors can get a taste of the fun—and hard work—involved in running such a high-caliber family business at the Annual Harvest Grape Stomp Festival in the fall.

PRODUCTION HIGHLIGHTS: Renowned for Baco Noir and Cabernet Francs.

Brimstone Hill Vineyard

CLAIM TO FAME: France by way of Pine Bush.

NOTES: Launched in 1969 on a half-acre slope, Richard and Valerie Eldridge channel Valerie's family history of winemaking in the Loire Valley of France, expanding slowly but surely and currently producing about ten thousand bottles a year on ten acres.

PRODUCTION HIGHLIGHTS: Hybrid and vinifera varietals, most notably their sparklers created in the tradition of French champagne.

Brotherhood Winery

CLAIM TO FAME: The founding father.

NOTES: America's oldest continuously operating winery—through Prohibition no less—the winery has always been firmly rooted in the past, with a village of nineteenth-century buildings, sunny courtyards and one of the biggest hand-excavated underground cellars in America.

PRODUCTION HIGHLIGHTS: Grapes are sourced from their vineyards and all over the state, with standout Riesling from the Finger Lakes and Pinot Noir from the Hudson Valley.

Brunel & Rafael Winery

CLAIM TO FAME: Only *Vitis vinifera* wine.
NOTES: These winemakers have opened their century-old home to visitors in Marlboro. This is probably the closest visitors will ever get to getting a glimpse at the heart and soul of a winemaker.
PRODUCTION HIGHLIGHTS: Spicy Cabernet Franc, barrel-fermented Chardonnay.

Clearview Vineyard

CLAIM TO FAME: Labor of love.
NOTES: These guys are fairly new, but they are serious: they made their first ten bottles of Cayuga White wine in 2008 and have increased their production every year.
PRODUCTION HIGHLIGHTS: Estate-grown hand-bottled wine sold in a tasting room that looks and feels more like your fantasy rec room than a winery. Bonus: amazingly good snacks are served with the wines.

Demarest Hill Winery & Distillery

CLAIM TO FAME: Little Italy in Warwick.
NOTES: The winery was created by Francesco Ciummo, who spent his youth tending his family's vineyard in Molise, Italy, learning the art and business of winemaking.
PRODUCTION HIGHLIGHTS: In 1994, he started producing single varietal and blended wine and now issues about four hundred cases per year.

Glorie Farm Winery

CLAIM TO FAME: Farm to bottle.
NOTES: The vineyard in Marlboro has an elevation of eight hundred feet, southeastern slopes, panoramic thirty-five-mile views of the valley and dozens of varieties of grapes in the ground.
PRODUCTION HIGHLIGHTS: Fifty-four-acre fruit farm the winemakers also tap into for some of their vibrant wines.

Palaia Vineyards & Winery

CLAIM TO FAME: Rock 'n' roll.
NOTES: With a two-hundred-year-old barn located five miles away from Woodbury Commons, live music on a forty-foot stage on the weekends, gourmet food and a robust social media presence, this ten-acre vineyard may not be able to compete in terms of production with the big boys, but it certainly can in terms of quirky commercial appeal.
PRODUCTION HIGHLIGHTS: Palaia has eight award-winning wines that run the gamut from crisp and dry to sweet and are food friendly (great for pairing with their imaginative menu of salads, sandwiches, pizzas and desserts). They also have two phenomenal house-made meads.

Robibero Winery

CLAIM TO FAME: Laid-back newbies.
NOTES: Robibero is the newest kid on Shawangunk's block, and with its spacious concrete bar, flat-screen TV, fireplace, outdoor fire pit and child- and pet-friendly policies, it still sports serious winery bona fides.
PRODUCTION HIGHLIGHTS: The winemaker at Robibero, Kristop Brown, hails from Benmarl, and his magic touch is palpable. The Traminette and Rabbit's Foot (blend of Baco Noir, Merlot and Cabernet Sauvignon) are spectacular.

Stoutridge Vineyard

CLAIM TO FAME: Slow wine.
NOTES: Stoutridge is on a ridge of land that has been home to grapevines and fruit trees for more than two hundred years. It was built on a vineyard planted in the late 1700s and was home to wineries and bootleg distilleries during Prohibition.
PRODUCTION HIGHLIGHTS: The winemakers create wines that have not been filtered, pumped or fined, allowing gravity to do the work of settling wines, which takes a lot longer than machines, but proponents say the method increases the level of antioxidants and complexity of flavor.

Warwick Valley Winery and Distillery

CLAIM TO FAME: Dirty (in a good way).
NOTES: The winery/distillery produces a beloved array of wines, liquors and ciders, all of which seek to express the variety of flavors the valley's rich and fertile soil produces. Their post-and-beam tasting room also allows visitors to explore not only their wines but also house-made ciders, brandies and liqueurs. Renovated from an apple-packing house, the tasting room overlooks a goose pond and orchards.
PRODUCTION HIGHLIGHTS: Our favorites include the Cabernet Sauvignon, Cabernet Franc and Pinot Gris. Fantastic strawberry wine as well.

Whitecliff Vineyard

CLAIM TO FAME: Artistes.
NOTES: With more than twenty varieties of grapes in the ground, this vineyard has a bucketful of accolades and fans (including top restaurants in New York City, an aberration for Hudson Valley wines).
PRODUCTION HIGHLIGHTS: Vineyards, a spacious tasting room and the family-friendly vibe make it a favorite across the board.

THE DUTCHESS WINE TRAIL

The Dutchess Wine Trail couldn't be more different than the Shawangunk. With just two wineries on the trail, it is 100 percent manageable for a day trip and an opportunity to take a farm-cation through the region's horse and dairy farms, woodlands, lakes, streams and historical mansions and estates.

Clinton Vineyards

CLAIM TO FAME: Classic French.
NOTES: The vineyard was established in 1976 by the late Ben Feder, a New York artist who spent time in France under the GI Bill and wanted to re-create the estate experience in Dutchess County.

PRODUCTION HIGHLIGHTS: His first effort, created in the French method champenoise, sold out. After his death, the tradition of top-selling premium wines has continued.

Millbrook Winery

CLAIM TO FAME: Critical darling. Established in 1984, Millbrook has been garnering critical acclaim ever since.

PRODUCTION HIGHLIGHTS: About fourteen thousand cases are produced per year. It is one of the most widely distributed Hudson Valley wines, with estate-grown fruit as well as grapes shipped from all over the state and as far away as California—a controversial move according to some, but one that has not diminished its diverse fan base or awarded winemaking.

THE UPPER HUDSON VALLEY WINE TRAIL

The Upper Hudson Valley Wine Trail, with wineries sprawling from Grandma Moses country in Washington County to the downtown bustle and sleek horse-race capital Saratoga, is the most philosophically, culturally and geographically diverse—and arguably, the least traditional wine trail. It is almost certainly the one least likely to pass the hardcore Hudson Valley sniff test.

Adirondack Winery

CLAIM TO FAME: Family affair.

NOTES: Launched in 2008 by Mike and Sasha Pardy, they have two young children who came along just as the nascent winery was launching. Considering the family's own demographics, the winery itself has a come-one-come-all child-friendly atmosphere, and their products are fun and festive.

PRODUCTION HIGHLIGHTS: Many feature berries besides grapes, like strawberries and blueberries.

Amorici Vineyard

CLAIM TO FAME: Sustainable New York.
NOTES: A farm winery, Amorici engages in sustainable farming practices and natural processing.
PRODUCTION HIGHLIGHTS: All grapes are grown in New York State, but primarily from the Finger Lakes and Long Island farms, not the Hudson Valley.

Fossil Stone Vineyards

CLAIM TO FAME: Horse farm turned vineyard.
NOTES: Fossil Stone Vineyards is a 150-acre horsing farm that dates back to 1802. A few horses remain, but now the crop that has risen from the loamy soil is grapes. After years of traveling the world, winemakers Michael and Kelly Spiak have turned to winemaking.
PRODUCTION HIGHLIGHTS: They are not currently open for tastings, but they do have harvest and other gathering events. In September of 2016, with a lot of help from visitors and friends, the winery harvested 4,933 pounds of Lacrescent grapes yielding 1,050 liters of juice.

Johnston's Winery

CLAIM TO FAME: High-quality imports.
NOTES: They source fruit, honey and grapes from California and New York to make wines, meads, jams and jellies. Honey and maple syrup and winemaking kits and brewing kits for home producers are also available.
PRODUCTION HIGHLIGHTS: The variety of fruit wines they make available—from grape to strawberry, cherry and, yes, even a dry blueberry—makes it an especially fun stop in the summer.

Ledge Rock Hill Winery & Vineyard

CLAIM TO FAME: Excellent dry and sweet selections.
NOTES: Located in the foothills of the Adirondacks, the family-run winery produces wines that embrace the sweet and dry side.
PRODUCTION HIGHLIGHTS: Chardonnay, Petite Sirah and Marquette wines are some of our favorite dry offerings on tap at Ledge Rock.

Natural Selection Farm Vineyard

CLAIM TO FAME: Foodie favorite.
NOTES: The winery's frost-friendly Burgundy-style reds, grown on site, are extremely food friendly with notes of spice.
PRODUCTION HIGHLIGHTS: No hints of sweetness here.

Northern Star Vineyard

CLAIM TO FAME: Gallery-winery.
NOTES: The winery's tasting room has free Wi-Fi, a laid-back group of knowledgeable staff members and a rotating gallery of contemporary artwork (for sale). They also happen to make wine grown and bottled at the vineyard.
PRODUCTION HIGHLIGHTS: Expect terroir-friendly reds like Frontenac and Marquette and whites like Prairie Star and Lacrosse.

Oliva Vineyards

CLAIM TO FAME: Horsey.
NOTES: With a horse race and grapes splashed across the logo, Oliva's wines literally wouldn't exist without horses. The horse-racing founders were such avid lovers of Saratoga—and wine—that they built a winery.
PRODUCTION HIGHLIGHTS: What the owners lack in wine pedigree is made up for in their passion for locally grown grapes and wine.

Saratoga Winery

CLAIM TO FAME: Cool kids.
NOTES: With live music, trivia nights, pasta dinners and a rustic Adirondack-style tasting bar (not to mention a picture of a reclining—tipsy?—horse on the logo), these hobbiest winemakers turned pros are as ready to chill as your favorite roommate in college.
PRODUCTION HIGHLIGHTS: Just with way better wine, most of which is sourced from the Finger Lakes.

Swedish Hill Winery

CLAIM TO FAME: Empire.
NOTES: In 1969, the Peterson family started farming grapes for other wineries and grew from there to encompass three wineries (Swedish Hill produces sixty thousand cases per year, while Goose Watch on Cayuga Lake and Penguin Bay on the Seneca Lake Wine Trail are smaller) and three tasting rooms, one of which is in Saratoga on this wine trail.
PRODUCTION HIGHLIGHTS: Most grapes are sourced from the Finger Lakes.

Thirsty Owl Saratoga

CLAIM TO FAME: Downtowners.
NOTES: The Thirsty Owl operates a vineyard and winery on the shores of Cayuga Lake, producing cool-climate grapes destined to be savored on the patio with carefully wine-paired food in downtown Saratoga—or in Cayuga Lake.
PRODUCTION HIGHLIGHTS: There's always a lot going on here, from live music to special tasting dinners. The Pinot Noir is especially beloved.

Victory View Vineyard

CLAIM TO FAME: Estate grown.
NOTES: The family-run operation grows, harvests and bottles all of its own French American hybrid grapes.
PRODUCTION HIGHLIGHTS: The tasting room is tiny, but the genuine celebration of farm-to-bottle wines and dedication is worth the visit.

THE HUDSON–BERKSHIRE BEVERAGE TRAIL

The Hudson-Berkshire Beverage Trail is more than just vino, featuring wines, craft beer, liquor and cider, sprawling across the Hudson Valley and the Berkshires, but don't let the disparate elements fool you. Though the trail is somewhat new in essence and definitely post-millennial in spirit, in many ways, it best embodies the current craft-DIY-local-everything zeitgeist that has taken possession of the American imagination.

Brookview Station Winery

CLAIM TO FAME: Apples.
NOTES: Located at Goold Orchards, the winery offers wines made from grapes and other fruits grown on-site. Not traditional, but that hasn't stopped the awards from rolling in for everything from their orchards.
PRODUCTION HIGHLIGHTS: Both apple and pear wines have been added to their traditional grape-centric drinks.

Furnace Brook Winery

CLAIM TO FAME: Sporty.
NOTES: This orchard-vineyard boasts apple-picking, hiking, cross-country skiing and, yes, snowshoeing on-site (which just happens to be in Massachusetts).
PRODUCTION HIGHLIGHTS: Their Pinot Grigio is one of their newer offerings, but its lightness, crispness and sweet profile make it a great pairing for rich New York cheeses.

Harvest Spirits

CLAIM TO FAME: Vodka. Made from New York apples.
NOTES: Founded in 2008 at Golden Harvest Farms between the Catskill and Berkshire Mountains, the distillery is equal parts modern tech marvel and homegrown love. It's where the farm meets urbanity in the form of delicious small-batch vodka, applejack, whiskey and brandy, all made from homegrown (or very close by) farm-fresh fruit.

Harvest Spirits next generation Derek Grout of Golden Harvest Orchards serves local libations at the HOOT! *Courtesy of FarmOnFoundation.org.*

PRODUCTION HIGHLIGHTS: The vodka is Harvest's most beloved product, but we have a soft spot for the Rare Pear Brandy and perennial harvest party-fave Cornelius Applejack.

Hudson-Chatham Winery

CLAIM TO FAME: Boutique Hudson Valley.

NOTES: This winery is as obsessed with the Hudson Valley's agriculture, literature, art, culture and history as it is with its grapes. In addition to opening the first winery in Columbia County, the DeVito family has created an agricultural haven with local cheeses, desserts, a restored 1780 farmhouse and a gazebo.

PRODUCTION HIGHLIGHTS: Their roster of wines celebrates and features a variety of grapes that flourish in the Hudson Valley.

Hudson Valley Distillers

CLAIM TO FAME: Whiskey.

NOTES: Founded by fraternity brothers Thomas Yozzo and Chris Meyer, the whiskey, vodka and applejack are all deliciously served from their 150-year-old lovingly restored big red barn.

PRODUCTION HIGHLIGHTS: The Adirondack Applejack, aged in white oak like an American whiskey, is smoother and subtler than most.

As you can see, there really is something for everyone, especially locavores, hikers, wine aficionados, architecture geeks, red barn lovers, winos toting toddlers and partying singles looking to mingle on the trail.

5

THE ROOTS

What does the Hudson Valley taste like? Can something that seems subjective ever be objectively answered? In its purest distillation, terroir is the taste of a place. So when a wonk says a wine expresses terroir beautifully, it means that, if it's a wine from Burgundy, it tastes just the way a wine from Burgundy should taste.

Seems simple. Except who defines what a region's wine should taste like, and how do they go about delivering the perfect, sought-after tasting notes? In the case of Burgundy, it's pretty straightforward. Burgundy, one of the most well-regarded wine-growing regions in France, has centuries of experience growing Pinot Noir (red Burgundy are made from 100 percent Pinot Noir grapes) and Chardonnay (white Burgundy are made from 100 percent Chardonnay grapes).

Burgundy wines are consistently the most highly rated varietals in the world, and they continue to command the highest prices in the market. Much of that fanatical devotion is due to the region's reputation for growing wines that express the beautiful vagaries of that particular microclimate in France.

Generally, wine regulations (and food regulations) are much stricter in France—at least on the surface—than wine regulations elsewhere. In Burgundy, the vines have become such an essential part of the country's identity as the avatar of all things delicious, grand and rarified that they are classified into four separate categories: Grand Cru (the highest rating, about 2 percent of wines from Burgundy), Premiere Cru (about 12 percent of wines), Village Wines (produced from grapes sourced from several vineyards in one of the forty-two villages in the region, about 36 percent of wines produced) and Regional (wines created from a variety of vineyards in more than one village, about 50 percent of wines created). The classifications always appear on the wine's label.

Like wines of Burgundy, wines created in most other well-regarded regions, like Champagne, Napa Valley, Willamette Valley or Barolo, also have certain notes or layers of complexity that let the drinker know they're not just drinking a wine from a familiar place, they're drinking a better wine from that region.

But when the average drinker picks up a Hudson Valley wine, most would be hard-pressed to define what they're expecting, and if forced to hazard a guess, it is unlikely that the description promises anything with the potential to earn a rave review from Robert Parker and Jancis Robinson.

"What people don't realize is that the Hudson Valley is the birthplace of American winemaking and viticulture," explained Carlo DeVito, prolific writer and publishing executive, co-founder of the Hudson-Berkshire Beverage Trail and co-owner of Hudson-Chatham Winery, among many other laudable things. "We have the oldest continually operating winery in North America at Brotherhood Winery in Washingtonville, and Benmarl is home to the oldest continually operating vineyard in the United States, as it is located on the old Caywood Estate, which has been continuously growing grapes since the mid-1800s."

But what does that mean?

Grapes grew wild in the Hudson Valley well before colonists arrived, according to DeVito. In fact, wild grapes may have earned North America the sobriquet Vinland when the Norseman Leif Ericsson reputedly stumbled on our shores in 1000 CE. The growing conditions for grapes, after all, are ideal when cultivated and curated in a proven practice.

"Gouged out by the icy finger of the Wisconsin ice sheet as it withdrew across the east coast of the continent, the Hudson Valley is riddled with little micro-climates, odd little eddies of warm water and swirling air, which help growers of all kinds in the valley," DeVito explained. "The Hudson Valley is bounded by the Palisades and the Shawangunks in the lower portion and swims between the Catskills and the foothills of the Taconic and Berkshire Mountains. The river provides a microclimate of its own much like the Finger Lakes. You have to remember that the Hudson River is a tidal river; we get a constant flow of air and water coming up from New York and down the river from north of Albany. These little pockets of heat and breeze are perfect for growing grapes. We can grow beautiful fruit in this valley, where we also grow apples, wheat, peaches and many other fruits and vegetables. It is truly a bountiful place."

But despite the fact that there are several species of grapes that are indigenous to the Hudson Valley, several European varieties grow well here (not to mention hybrids of native and European grapes) and the wine industry in the Empire State is only behind California and Washington in terms of production, the few Americans outside of New York who have tried wines from our region have done so almost accidentally, as a little side stopover on a general tour of the Hudson Valley. (Unless, of course, they are among the growing ranks of avid wine drinkers who subscribe to wine magazines and are constantly on the search for the next, best up-and-coming wine regions.)

Partially, that's due to the diminutive size of our production. With 500 acres under vine, several dozen wineries generally produce 400 to 1,500 cases per year here, versus the size of, say, Napa's production, with 45,158 acres under vine, 789 wineries and an estimated 49.7 million cases of wine produced annually. The market reach hampers the Hudson Valley region's ability to define itself on a grand scale.

There's more to it than just geographical logistics though.

The Empire State Grape embodies everything we love about this great state: beauty, toughness, deliciousness and complexity. Reprinted with permission from *Grapes of the Hudson Valley and Other Cool Climate Regions of the United States and Canada* by J. Stephen Casscles. *Courtesy of Flint Mine Press.*

The Hudson Valley wine world is populated, notoriously—for better and, in same cases, definitely worse—by hardy individualists who were attracted to the Hudson Valley's fertile land. Primarily, they are grape growers from afar without capital or roots or second-careerists who hoped to make a unique mark on the industry by growing, harvesting and producing the grapes. The result is a heterogeneous mix of grape varieties. It's next to impossible to settle on a definitive number of varieties being grown because enterprising institutions like Cornell University are always innovating and experimenting with new hybrid grape varietals.

"We give promising varieties to growers to tinker with," Chris Gerling, a leading grape growing expert at Cornell University, explained. "Our goal is to find grapes that can deal with late freezes in the spring, early freezes in the fall, variable humidity, with characteristics that meet or exceed what is currently available taste-wise, but with better disease resistance and hardiness." Some consumers resist hybrids because they've never heard of them—cultivated to naturally resist disease, environmental challenges and pests, they require less chemical spraying and are much "greener" to grow than the so-called noble varieties.

Environmentally conscious and economically aware farmers are eager to grow the tastiest new grapes in their fields. Grape varieties that grow in the Hudson Valley include white and pink natives, red natives, white French hybrids, red French hybrids, New York hybrids, white vinifera varieties and red vinifera varieties. Because the Hudson Valley is one of America's oldest wine regions and has always attracted the intelligent, with an independent streak and something to prove, the grapes in the vineyards are more diverse in the Hudson Valley than anywhere else in the world.

Before we talk grape varietals though, we have to talk land. Because how the Hudson Valley is delineated is another subject of contention.

In the 1980s, the federal government set out to compete with France's much-lauded *appellation d'origine contrôlée* (AOC). The system basically designates and legally controls geographically based names of wine (Champagne), food (Camembert) and spirits (Cognac). The system was designed to prevent charlatans from marketing products created in another region with a pilfered concept. It is honored not only in France but also in Europe and elsewhere; the system works for many other reasons, including economic development.

The AOC was developed in the early twentieth century to combat fraud and adulteration and deal with the fallout of the microscopic vineyard pest named phylloxera that eats grape roots and was responsible for essentially wiping out more than 70 percent of the vines in France in the late 1800s. The AOC incentivized growers and producers in areas where traditional grape varieties flourish from cultivating hybrid grapes that might be cheaper and easier to grow. The guidelines are sometimes laughably exacting and precise and even go so far as to regulate maximum yields, vine age, vine density and pruning techniques.

It respects natural boundaries imposed by geography, culture and tradition and allows farmers and producers to make a sustainable living and fair living wage.

But like the rote memorization and deadpan recitation of the multiplication table and the table of chemical elements we were forced to learn and robotically regurgitate in elementary school, the system, while effective, can arguably stymie creativity, scientific innovation, questioning and, quite frankly, plain ol' delicious American fun.

In the 1980s, the Bureau of Alcohol, Tobacco and Firearms developed its own Americanized version, dubbed the American Viticultural Area (AVA). The AVA defines regions by geographic boundaries, and there are no restrictions regarding types of grapes planted or their yields. The sizes of the regions vary dramatically, from 29,900 square miles across four states (the Upper Mississippi Valley AVA) to the Cold Ranch AVA in California, at 189 acres. To receive an AVA designation, the name of the proposed area must be recognized regionally *or* nationally, and it must be proven that growing conditions (elevation, type of soil, the climate) are distinctive.

To officially use an AVA designation, wineries have to have utilized 85 percent of AVA-grown grapes, with only 15 percent from other sources. And if the wine label also indicates a specific varietal or type of grape, 75 percent must come from the AVA-designated source.

Officially, the Hudson Valley AVA was established in 1982. The area sprawls over 224,000 acres. Only about 500 of those are currently planted. The rolling Gunks and the Hudson River insulate grapes from some of mother nature's more bipolar extremes, and the Hudson Valley Wine & Grape Association has set up strict bylaws governing what they define as Hudson Heritage White Wine and Hudson Heritage Red Wine.

While every winery can produce its own version, and each will taste different depending on the location of the vineyard, harvesting practices and creative choices the winemaker makes when fermenting and aging the juice, it is an attempt à la France to ensure consistency and quality. It is also a savvy marketing move.

THE OFFICIAL RULES

Hudson Heritage White

All grapes must be sourced from the Hudson Valley AVA
The following grapes may be used:
  Seyval 70–85 percent

The rest of the blend may consist of any or all of the following:
  Vidal
  Vignoles
  Cayuga
  Traminette
  Up to 2 percent residual sugar
  No malolactic fermentation
  No oak, barrels, chips, staves
  Hock-style bottle

Hudson Heritage Red

All grapes must be sourced from the Hudson Valley AVA
The following grapes may be used:
  Norict 35 55 percent
  Dechaunac 35–55 percent
  Other hybrid 20–30 percent
  Oak aging is allowed
  Residual Sugar <=1.0 percent
  Malolactic fermentation allowed
  TA <.8 gms./100ml, VA <75, pH <3.8
  Burgundy-style bottle

For those who are familiar with Michael Migliore and his tireless work as the winemaker at Whitecliff and his generous offers of help to newbie winemakers in the valley, it is no surprise that not only is he president of the association, but he also helped craft the bylaws, which, while strict, allow for just enough wiggle room to ensure that the unique fingerprint of every vineyard's terroir will be tasted in every sip.

The fact is though, these days, a fifth-grade recitation of the periodic table has about as much impact on our lives as the AVA has on New York State wineries. It's in the back of our minds, somewhere we simultaneously revisit and appreciate, understanding the importance of a substance's chemical properties abstractly. Certainly, we don't organize life around it, and most Hudson Valley–area winemakers couldn't care less whether the AVA considers their status official or not.

The second half of the twentieth century was a slow and painful climb back to relative relevance and prosperity for the wine industry in New York. Before Prohibition, the Hudson Valley was a vibrant and productive home to grape growers and winemakers alike. But Prohibition annihilated the region, and with a few exceptions (notably, Brotherhood, which sold communion wine to churches), the growers turned to other crops to make a living.

The Hudson Valley entered a dark, not to mention decidedly less relaxing period of winemaking. Even when Prohibition was overturned on December 5, 1933, growers were loath to start over again.

Until the 1970s, there were just a handful of wineries in the Hudson Valley, despite the fact that it is home to the oldest continuously operating winery in North America (Brotherhood Winery, which began production in 1839) and the oldest continuously cultivated vineyard (since 1677, now home to Benmarl Winery). The '70s were a turning point for the region. New York's governor, Hugh Carey, appointed John Dyson to be the commissioner of agriculture. Dyson has been widely credited (along with Mark Miller of Benmarl) as a driving force in the establishment of the Farm Winery Act of 1976, which vastly reduced costs of creating and operating a winery and allowed grape growers in New York to establish a winery and sell directly to the public, as long as their take doesn't exceed 190,000 liters annually.

And then on June 4, 1982, the Hudson Valley AVA was created.

Very few Hudson Valley wineries use the AVA designation on their labels. This is partially due to the complete lack of interest consumers seem to have in the AVA and its goings-on (in direct opposition to France, where major violations of the AOC can result in front-page news stories as widely recognized as presidential election coverage in the United States).

While many Hudson Valley wineries blithely operate without thinking twice about the AVA, many believe the designation helped drive tourism and the slow-building but rallying regional wine revolution.

Officially, the designated area encompasses Columbia, Dutchess and Putnam Counties.

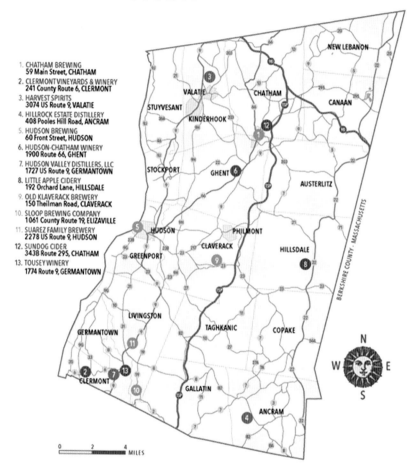

map to
Artisanal Beverage Makers in
COLUMBIA COUNTY

1. CHATHAM BREWING
   59 Main Street, CHATHAM
2. CLERMONT VINEYARDS & WINERY
   241 County Route 6, CLERMONT
3. HARVEST SPIRITS
   3074 US Route 9, VALATIE
4. HILLROCK ESTATE DISTILLERY
   408 Pooles Hill Road, ANCRAM
5. HUDSON BREWING
   60 Front Street, HUDSON
6. HUDSON-CHATHAM WINERY
   1900 Route 66, GHENT
7. HUDSON VALLEY DISTILLERS, LLC
   1727 US Route 9, GERMANTOWN
8. LITTLE APPLE CIDERY
   192 Orchard Lane, HILLSDALE
9. OLD KLAVERACK BREWERY
   150 Theilman Road, CLAVERACK
10. SLOOP BREWING COMPANY
    1061 County Route 19, ELIZAVILLE
11. SUAREZ FAMILY BREWERY
    2278 US Route 9, HUDSON
12. SUNDOG CIDER
    343B Route 295, CHATHAM
13. TOUSEY WINERY
    1774 Route 9, GERMANTOWN

Dive into local libations, history and farm-to-table cuisine in beautiful Columbia County.
Courtesy of Columbia County Tourism.

According to the mandate, the area begins where the Merritt Parkway crosses the New York–Connecticut state line and heads north along the Columbia-Rensselaer County line to the Columbia-Greene County line along the Hudson River. It then proceeds south along the Columbia-Greene County line in the river to the northeast corner of Ulster County, where it heads west along the Ulster-Greene County line to Route 214.

Then it heads south on the eastern side of 214 to the junction with Route 28 in Phoenicia. From there, the line meanders south along Route 28 until it hits 28A, where it continues down the road toward Samonsville. From there, it weaves through Tacasco, Mombaccus, Fantinekill and Pataukunk to Route 209, where it continues along the eastern side of the route to the New York–Pennsylvania state line in the Delaware River. It makes a turn and heads east along the Delaware until it bumps up against the New York–New Jersey state line at Route 17.

Then it goes north along the west side of Route 17 until it hits Interstate 287, where it heads east along the northern side of 287 until it hits the Merritt Parkway, at which point it proceeds easterly along the Taconic Parkway until it circles back to its starting point.

Most vineyards are planted within two miles of the Hudson River. The early morning sunshine hits the western side of the river first, and many vineyards are planted there to capitalize on those extra morning rays. The river also helps moderate some of the harsher Hudson Valley arctic blasts and summer scorchers, bathing vines in cooling summer breezes and warmer maritime temps in the winter; the moderating weather is sent up the river from the Atlantic Ocean.

The total wine cultivation area is 224,000 acres, with approximately 500 acres planted with vines. (Compare that to about 45,000 acres of vines in Napa Valley.)

There are wineries that consider themselves to be Hudson Valley wineries and don't officially fit within the parameters of the AVA and wine trails that are recognized by outsiders to be "Hudson Valley" wine trails for their comparable terrain, soil and climate that are not officially 100 percent within the boundaries of the AVA either. For even serious oenophiles, sommeliers and wine critics, they're Hudson Valley wine trails, and for our practical purposes, they are too.

But while the old guard values rival or resent frisky new upstart wineries and trails popping up off the grid, the practice of winemaking perseveres with the pride of New York only a New Yorker understands.

Hudson Valley wineries can be roughly divided into three regions: the Upper Hudson Valley, the Middle Hudson Valley and the Lower Hudson Valley. Unlike the AVA, the National Heritage map as defined by New York State claims the Hudson Valley covers four million acres stretching from the town of Waterford in Saratoga County to the city of Yonkers in Westchester.

There were thirty-six farm wineries in the Hudson Valley at last count, according to the Department of Ag, which sounds like a lot, but

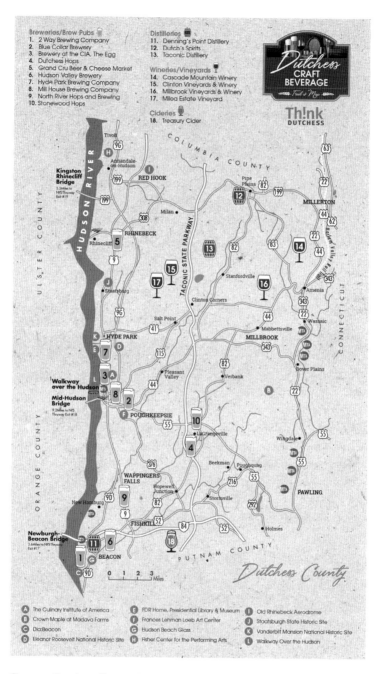

Come to Dutchess County for the wine, stay for the food, culture and history. *Courtesy of Dutchess County Tourism.*

considering the vast size of the region, it makes what we have been taught to expect from a day on the wine trail less practical.

Instead, exploring wineries in the Hudson Valley offers an opportunity for oenophiles to not only have a few great drinks but also to truly immerse themselves in the land, people and climate that create these magical elixirs. Wine tourism is ripe for a millennial-style upgrade, and some winemakers are picking up on this. Turn to Appendix C for a guide to wine festivals in the Hudson Valley.

Three Varieties of Grapes Grown in the Hudson Valley

Native or Labrusca Varieties

Native and labrusca are used interchangeably among scientists, grape growers and winemakers—it just means they evolved in Hudson Valley soil. The first wines made in the region were made from *Vitis labrusca* grapes. While their flavor (sweet and musty) isn't ideal for our current palate, the fact that they evolved here means they can withstand the weather and pests that are also indigenous to the region. In the 1800s, scientists started experimenting with crossing the native grapes with French grapes to help fight the phylloxera and grape epidemics that devastated France, and the legacy of those experiments can also be found throughout the Hudson Valley's vineyards. Today, one native grape used in commercial winemaking is thought to be all labrusca. Others, like Niagara, Catawba and Diamond, are mostly labrusca with a dash of vinifera.

Hybrid (French American) Varieties

Most of the hybrids used in the region were developed by French scientists working between 1880 and 1950. The horticulturalists toiled away, creating hybrids of natives and viniferas in an attempt to find the perfect disease-resistant but delicious grape flavor. But around the same time, with farming technology improvements, including the development of more powerful insecticides and fungicides, many growers pulled out of the hybrid and native businesses and begin planting primarily vinifera varietals. The growers in the Hudson Valley were bowing to perceived consumer demand, and that decision probably had long-lasting implications for the industry. Vinifera simply won't grow as well here as it will in California, and farmers have to add a lot more fortifiers to the soil to coax grapes to grow at all.

Vinifera (European) Varieties

Vinifera is to wine like Chanel is to fashion—the best quality and most expensive and sophisticated choice in the industry. Vinifera species (there are hundreds of them) are beloved because they're classic, dependable workhorses that deliver what the consumer wants (in a word, yum). Vinifera are native to the Black Sea and spread throughout Europe through careful cultivation. The earliest attempts to plant vinifera in the Hudson Valley were a bust, but they still account for the vast majority (over 95 percent) of the wine cultivated.

These days, what we're growing in the Hudson Valley is a hodgepodge of natives and vinifera, with an emphasis—for now—on hybrids. What we discussed above bears repeating: there are probably several dozen other wine-grape hybrids being planted in vineyards around the valley. The visionary, scientist and innovator-farmer Michael Migliore of Whitecliff Winery has spoken on several occasions about the small batches of experimental hybrids he grows in his vineyard, many so new and untried they don't have names, just numbers.

And he isn't alone. Chris Gerling of the grape-wine program at Cornell University works with several Hudson Valley growers on experimental plantings, and Michael works one-on-one with growers and winemakers across the Hudson Valley to help them marry the art and science of growing grapes in our difficult climate.

And yes, while it's tempting to romanticize the art of grape growing from afar, in the vineyard, it's essential to monitor how humidity, drainage and temporal fluctuations can affect every different species of grapes—while ever conscious of the budget, manpower and acreage (or lack thereof) that most growers have access to. Winemakers in the Hudson Valley simply don't have the luxury of operating in a silo if they want to produce wines that can compete with less expensive vintages from afar.

And despite the challenge, or perhaps because of it, some of the most critically acclaimed wineries in the Hudson Valley are focusing exclusively on vinifera. Millbrook Vineyards, owned by Pebble Ridge Vineyard and

Estates, was the first to focus on vinifera exclusively. The founders of Pebble Ridge, John and Kathy Dyson, are devoted to producing the best wines that can flourish in the region they're produced in. (They have one thousand acres today—up from one in 1979—in California, Tuscany and the Hudson Valley.)

As the New York State commissioner of agriculture from 1975 to 1979 under Governor Hugh Carey's administration, Dyson toured New York vineyards, met pioneers like Dr. Konstantin Frank of the Finger Lakes and learned why and how some of the most daring growers were planting vinifera. (As commissioner, he is also credited, along with Benmarl founder Mark Miller, with the establishment of the Farm Winery Act of 1976, which vastly reduced costs of creating and operating a winery.) In consultation with Dr. Frank, Dyson decided to launch his own vinifera experiment on his father's farm in Millbrook.

Borrowing Dr. Frank's plow, he planted several varieties, played with rootstocks and trellising techniques and, through trial and error, proved that vinifera grapes could blossom here and, perhaps more importantly, be transformed into palate-pleasing wines.

In 1981, Dyson and David Bova decided to found a winemaking company—in Dyson's home garage. The company was dubbed Veraison Wine Cellars, and it referred to the moment when a grape ripens. The time for an innovative winery devoted to vinifera was also clearly ripe. They soon brought on fellow Cornell University alum John Graziano to make the wine. In 1985, they released their first vintage and, essentially, helped build the path for a sustainable economic future for Hudson Valley wine.

"I think grapes like Traminette and Baco Noir and Chelois are very palatable to the consumer," DeVito said. "The Baco Noir [varietals] of the Hudson Valley, such as Warwick Valley Black Dirt, and Hudson-Chatham Winery's numerous small production Baco Noir grapes, as well as several others that use it in their blends, make fabulous wines. Warwick and Hudson-Chatham Baco Noir wines are in stores and restaurants up and down the Hudson Valley and New York. And other Hudson Valley Baco Noir and Chelois are sold at a terrific rate at the Culinary Institute of America. NPR has compared Chelois to Pinot Noir from Burgundy."

Being compared to a Burgundy on NPR is the wine world equivalent of having *Vanity Fair* casually refer to a starlet as the "next Meryl Streep."

A few important critical successes, while deeply satisfying, don't do much to enrich the industry. In some ways, what defines Hudson Valley terroir is similar to what defines its culture: eccentricity, diversity and inclusion.

The 411 on Wine-Grape Varieties Commonly Planted in the Hudson Valley

SEYVAL BLANC: French American hybrid grape. Heavy producing white. Most widely planted white grape in the Hudson Valley that produces good sugar and acid balance. Usually blended with other varieties.

BACO NOIR: French American hybrid grape. Produces medium bodied, deeply tinted red wine with aromas of vanilla and chocolate and with good acid balance.

CHARDONNAY: French Vinifera grape. Fruity, with smoky vanilla and butter flavors and aromas if barrel fermented. Most widely planted vinifera grape in the Hudson Valley.

CABERNET FRANC: Red vinifera grape best suited for growing in the Hudson Valley. Produces a wine with soft tannins, good fruit with a peppery nose and usually found in Bordeaux-style blends.

PINOT NOIR: Medium-bodied red wine with aromas of black cherries, raspberries and currants.

GAMAY NOIR: Medium-bodied red wine that is a clone of Pinot Noir. French vinifera grape dating back to the fifteenth century. Produces a wine with elements of cherries and cranberries. Sometimes made into an early season Nouveau.

VIGNOLES: White wine that can be made into a dry wine or late harvest wine. Floral aromas and fruity flavors of pineapple and apricot.

RIESLING: A crisp white wine characterized by mineral and slate flavors with fruit notes of peaches and apricots when fully ripened.

GEWÜRZTRAMINER: White wine with spicy characteristics and floral aspects of lychee on the bouquet.

VIDAL: Full-body white, clean citrus flavors of lemon and grapefruit. Produce a good balanced wine that's paired well with seafood and poultry.

FRONTENAC: Full-body red grape, with cherry / plum aromas. High in sugar, heavy producing hybrid from University of Minnesota.

TRAMINETTE: A late mid-season white wine grape that produces wine with pronounced varietal character likened to one of its parents, Gewürztraminer. Traminette is distinguished by its superior wine quality combined with good productivity, partial resistance to several fungal diseases and cold hardiness superior to its acclaimed parent, Gewürztraminer. Traminette resulted from the cross, Joannes Seyve 23.416 x Gewürztraminer, developed in 1965 by H.C. Barrett.

A late-ripening French American hybrid, the Chelois grape, grown to great acclaim by the Hudson-Chatham Winery, inspiring other local growers to plant this beauty. Reprinted with permission from *Grapes of the Hudson Valley and Other Cool Climate Regions of the United States and Canada* by J. Stephen Casscles. *Courtesy of Flint Mine Press.*

Embracing the chaos and diffusion of the industry and accepting that it's part of the "charm" are as essential as Michael Migliore's laser-like attention to improving the scientific rigor used by winemakers and growers in the vineyard and production rooms.

Some Hudson Valley winemakers are taking terroir to a whole new level, utilizing products from the earth to underline or temper the effects of the climate on the grapes.

It would be difficult to find a more enthusiastic proponent of Hudson Valley's earth than Carlo DeVito. Taking his inspiration from a piece that Anne Zimmerman had written about a "Dirt Tasting" (participants were offered glasses of dirt and vegetables and wine made from grapes grown in that dirt) and the techniques utilized by Randall Grahm of Santa Cruz, California's Bonny Doon Vineyard (he dumped crushed rocks into his wine while it fermented to give it an extra layer of minerality), he decided to make Field Stone Baco Noir for Hudson-Chatham.

Carlo gathered and cleaned river stones from the vineyard and placed them in a tank that held Baco Noir Old Vines. He also gathered local oak tree limbs that had fallen years ago, milled them and dried them in a kiln and added the chips to the tank. He tried it after about a week and was horrified to primarily discover notes of "mud and moss." But, left without much of a choice, he persevered. Four months later, the wine was well rounded, with a deep minerality that spoke not only of the Hudson Valley land but also of his courage; pioneering, fearless spirit; and inquisitiveness.

Paul Deninno, owner and winemaker at Bashakill Vineyards, also goes to great lengths to embrace every element of the local terroir, even bringing in sheep to handle weeds and provide, well, their special brand of fertilizer. "It's organic and effective," he said, "not to mention eco-friendly, which is important to me as a producer, but also someone who lives right here. We also age our wines in natural caves, which we believe imbues them, naturally, with the perfect level of humidity and temperature control, without requiring a waste of energy."

The physical location of an aging facility—in addition to its temperature and level of humidity—can have an effect on the overall taste of the finished product, an effect that feels somehow more magic than science. Whiskey makers in Scotland with aging facilities near shallows in the sea are often thought to have superior products because of the remnants of tang from salty, mineral-rich air from algae-heavy low tides that some say can be detected in Bruichladdich, for example.

The Hudson Valley's resident terroir obsessives are Stoutridge's Stephen Osborn and Kim Wagner.

"Some people really like to drill down and talk about micro-climates in terroir from vineyard to vineyard, but I like to think about it more like a two- or three-mile swath," Stephen said. "Here in Marlboro, there's us, Benmarl and Glorie. We grow some of our grapes on their vineyards. I like to think of the mezoclimate in Marlboro radiating from the land as the mountains slip into the great Hudson River."

Instead of focusing on how, say, Seyval Blanc grown in his vineyard versus Seyval Blanc grown in another vineyard taste in a glass side by side, Stephen is more interested in finding a new grape that will grow just as well as Seyval Blanc, but perhaps adding another layer of terroir expression.

Stephen and Kim experiment with different plantings, all with an eye on what could possibly—or already has at some point, but doesn't currently in abundance—flourish in the Hudson Valley.

The winemaking techniques they employ are purely biological in nature. Stephen and Kim rely on the grapes to ferment and resolve any rough edges or flaws in the tank—flaws that are commonly dealt with through chemistry but that the natural winemaking process eschews.

"If you give it a chance, nature takes care of a lot," Stephen explains. "Because we don't introduce chemicals or additives, we don't create new problems to resolve old ones. If you give wine time, it will express itself more genuinely on its own than the modern finishing process will allow it to."

He likens conventional wine to a beautiful painting of the night sky and natural wine to the night sky itself. "When Van Gogh saw the night sky that became his gorgeous painting *The Starry Night*, there was a process of re-creating it," Stephen says. "First he had to look it at, then he had to go to his studio to paint it from memory. He had to re-create it, brush stroke by brush

Hand-plucked grapes are the rule at vineyards in the Hudson Valley—no robo-pickers here! *Courtesy of the Hudson-Berkshire Beverage Trail.*

stroke. As beautiful as *The Starry Night* is, I love to bring people to the night sky and show them that."

Stephen and the increasingly successful natural wine movement assert that the art of stabilizing wine dilutes its nature.

He continued, "But don't get me wrong. Yes, I personally love natural wine and think everyone should at least be exposed to it. But I understand it's not practical, and a really great, locally produced finished wine that makes it to more people than mine ever will is a wonderful thing, and I'm all for it."

Stoutridge only sells wine on the premises, but it does a respectable business, cranking out about three thousand cases per year. Visitors who come to the tasting room get not only Stephen and Kim's pure evocation of Hudson Valley terroir but also insight into their philosophy and a crash course in what the heck makes natural wine so much more natural than plain old local farmhouse wine.

And whether you're reaching for Stoutridge or another Hudson Valley vintage, Stephen has some thoughts on the grapes that grow best here.

STEPHEN'S FAVORED WHITES

Seyval Blanc

"I adore it. I love the lightness of the flavor. I think light wines are able to express more complexity. Sometimes the more assertive wines have one or two flavors that become too dominant and drown out all of the nuance. Like a peppery stew. Seyval Blanc grown in the Hudson Valley—especially, I would argue, Marlboro—is wonderfully complex. You really taste the minerally terroir."

Vidal

"I do like what can be done with Vidal in the Hudson Valley. It's soft and what I would call almost pastel-y."

Niagara

"The Niagara wine we make here in the natural method has a very intense but subtle texture. I always recommend Niagara to anyone seeking a drier, subtle and complex wine that speaks of the Hudson Valley."

Stephen's Favored Reds

Cabernet Franc

"I love the movement to make it the signature grape of the Hudson Valley. I'm not growing it myself because everyone else is, but the folks who are growing it well and really understand Cab Franc are producing amazing, distinctive Hudson Valley wines that can't be produced anywhere else, even with the same grape."

Dechaunac

"This is one of the great underrated blending grapes. Blend it with a Cab Franc in the Hudson Valley that's grown well and you'll have a light, complex and spicy drinking red. Beautiful."

Frontenac

"Makes beautiful, intense wines. There is real umami in this wine if you let it ferment and really get a little weird. The range of flavors available with this grape, especially when you allow them to come forth naturally, is completely unique and truly outstanding."

Speaking with winemakers, it's easy to be persuaded that they're all operating in their own separate silos. While many admit that all too often it's true, there is a concerted effort to change that, with the theory that exchanging observations, ideas, successes and failures with their nominal winemaking competitors will, instead of diminishing their own product, lift up the entire industry in the Hudson Valley with a collective agreement that collaboration is the new business mentality.

Michael Migliore, the aforementioned founder and winemaker at the twenty-six-acre Whitecliff Winery, is a former chemical engineer and one of the most widely respected and social producers in the region. With his scientific background, apparently boundless energy and ambition to help the region carve out more than just a quirky outpost in the wine world, Migliore serves in an unofficial capacity as a consultant and advisor to new and old winemakers and grape growers in the Hudson Valley.

He founded the Hudson Valley Wine and Grape Association (HVWGA) to "increase the quality and quantity of wine and grape production in the Hudson Valley through education, knowledge, networking and cooperation."

Michael hosts informal get-togethers and blind tastings for winemakers and encourages both neophytes and old hands to talk shop. The HVWGA also established certain parameters for what, precisely, can qualify as a Hudson Heritage White and Hudson Heritage Red, as discussed on page 84.

The concept of marketing a heritage Hudson Valley red and white wine is genius and one that will—hopefully—help entice some of the New York restaurateurs who clamor for the farm-to-table region's meats, cheeses, fruit and vegetables to fall in love with local wine too. Until recently, most have snubbed the grapes.

The HVGWA isn't the only organization trying to leverage marketing prowess and grapes that show significant promise growing here to draw eyeballs and thirsty lips to the region. Doug and MaryEllen Glorie of Glorie Farm Winery and the publishers of *Hudson Valley Wine* magazine are collaborating on the Hudson Valley Cabernet Franc Coalition. (More on the publishers of the *Hudson Valley Wine* magazine in chapter 7 and Cabernet Franc in chapter 8.)

Cab Franc (as it is commonly called) first earned its reputation in Bordeaux, where it is utilized in red wine blends. But it grows gloriously all over the Hudson Valley, delivering a soft, lush finish with just a dash of bracing pepper. The Cab Franc Coalition, which comprises winemakers and growers, is partnering with the Hudson Valley Research Lab to find the most promising strains to plant. Their primary goal is to make Cab Franc the signature grape of the region.

But even if the campaigns to create Heritage Reds and Whites and make Cabernet Franc the signature grape are as successful as the founders (and we) hope they'll be, there's little risk of the Hudson Valley winemakers selling out to big wine.

Don't get us wrong. Big wine—much like big food—still has a vise-like grip on consumers' palates. American big wine regularly gulps up smaller producers, with just three companies—E&J Gallo, the Wine Group and Constellation Wines—totaling 187.5 million cases of the 370 million produced in 2013. Add the next three big boys—Bronco, Trinchero Family Estates and Treasury—and the top six are making 241.4 million cases, or two-thirds of the wine made in the United States.

Gallo, the biggest of the biggies, cranks out roughly eighty million cases. That's a lot of grape juice. (It's more than the bottom twenty-six in the top thirty produce all together.)

Back up ten years to 2003, and twelve of the producers in the top thirty have been absorbed into some of the larger companies.

Quite possibly the most important and unpredictable—and, therefore, nearly impossible to plan for minus the type of distribution and marketing network only large-scale manufacturers have access to—key to any label's success in the Hudson Valley or anywhere else is the consumer.

Take Australia's notoriously successful Yellow Tail. In the early 1990s, imports of Australian wine were nominal, hovering at about 3 percent. Flash forward to 2001, when Yellow Tail debuted and sold 200,000 cases. Not bad. But by the next year, Yellow Tail was selling 2.2 million worldwide, and currently it sells about 8 million cases—in the United States alone.

So, what is the magical formula for success? Money plus marketing, a distinct lack of shame and/or a moral compass?

Deutsch Family Wine and Spirits, also responsible for making Georges Duboeuf such a rollicking success in America, was looking for the next big, cheap thing. The goal was to introduce a cheap (less than ten dollars) bottle of wine that would please the American consumer. For a nation of soda and juice chuggers, that meant ripe, fruity-tooty, low-tannin, low-acid product, what most would refer to as alcoholic grape juice.

As the Deutsch CEO said in an interview with the wine blog VinePair, "We couldn't generate this kind of wine at the sub-ten-dollar price level out of France, so we decided to look to Australia."

Shiny new tanks soak up the history at Brotherhood Winery. *Courtesy of Brotherhood Winery.*

The company found a winemaking family (the Casellas) who were willing to play ball and grow grapes for the company. There have been vague accusations in the industry that Yellow Tail (like many other large-scale wine companies) tampers with the levels of acidity and tannins in the wine to deliver an even more quaffable, sweet sip for consumers. The accusations have never been proven.

In addition to going for notes of soda and orange juice, Yellow Tail aggressively marketed the wine with a cartoon-like kangaroo on its label—the first in the industry to push wine with a label that, on its face, would appeal to juveniles, now a common practice.

If Yellow Tail was setting out to appeal to high school kids, it couldn't have taken a more targeted approach. It's a cynical method of wine selling and one that refuses to challenge or educate consumers, setting out to intoxicate them, literally and metaphorically, with flashy graphics and an appeal to the lowest common denominator of their palates.

To put that in perspective, the biggest producer in the Hudson Valley, Brotherhood Winery, manages to put out about fifty thousand cases per year, and much of that is sourced from grapes outside of the Hudson Valley proper, in the Finger Lakes and on Long Island.

The Hudson Valley wine region will always be a series of small wineries bearing quirky grapes, staffed by individuals with sky-high ideals who just dream of making great wine, even if that requires sheep poop in a cave. And you know what? That makes it a safer, cleaner and much tastier place to visit, live and drink.

6

NON-GRAPE WINES

When you think wine, grapes are almost always implicitly part of the definition. Drinking non-grape wine feels like cheating somehow—like something that should be surreptitiously sipped by young adults before they know how to drink or what they can get their hands on—good, bad or ugly.

And when we do know (a little) better, the first thing we start exploring is what everyone (okay, so mostly older cousins and Instagram) tells us the "best wine is to try," which invariably includes the reality of cost. In other words, even if we're drinking American-made stuff, it is viewed and appreciated through the lens of Europe and our pocketbooks.

It can get complicated, especially when you want your wine to be not only homegrown but also locally grown. In the Hudson Valley, the deposit of shale, slate, schist and limestone over millennia gave great flavor to the soil, resulting in unfamiliar flavor profiles, even among the classic noble grapes.

Nobles are the grapes that are most commonly name-checked on every bestselling bottle at your local wine shop.

The six noble grapes, beloved for their ease of growth and/or the almost universal appreciation of their classically accepted taste, made them ubiquitous: Cabernet Sauvignon, Merlot, Pinot Noir, Chardonnay, Riesling and Sauvignon Blanc. Out of these six, all but Riesling were born in France (and Riesling was grown in the Alsace region of France almost from the get-go).

THE NOBLE ROOTS

Cabernet Sauvignon

An accidental cross between red Cabernet Franc and white Sauvignon Blanc grape in southwestern France yielded this extraordinarily durable, tannin-heavy, oak-friendly, full-bodied, food-friendly winner.

Merlot

Literally, it means the little blackbird. It is renowned for its soft, easy-drinking, food-friendly, highly approachable gateway grape status.

Pinot Noir

The film *Sideways* was devoted to this hard-to-grow Burgundy-born beauty with ripe red berry flavor and a muskiness that is often likened to "forest floor" by sommeliers. Food friendly but light in alcohol, it is often sipped solo.

Chardonnay

Also born in Burgundy, Chardonnay is often used in still and sparkling wines and has a reputation for embracing the terroir of an individual place better than any other grape. That said, depending on where it's grown, it can be ripe and tropical or earthy and apple-y.

Riesling

With the flavor of pitted fruits like apricots and peaches, coupled with crisp, acidic and dry notes, the grape is enjoyed for its yin and yang, dual nature. Born in Rhine, Germany, in the fifteenth century.

Sauvignon Blanc

Originating in Bordeaux, it is known for its grassy, crisp character and pucker-inducing low sugar levels.

It's apple-harvesting time at the family-run Goold Orchards farm. Going apple picking at family-owned farms is an absolute must in New York every fall. *Courtesy of Brookview Station Winery and Goold Orchards.*

The plots of land that can be planted in the Hudson Valley for grapes tend to be on the small side, making large-scale production wineries an impossibility for geographic reasons alone. In a map compiled by Cornell University in 1961, the types of soil lining the Hudson Valley are various, with medium to moderately coarse soils on glacial till and moderate to fine-textured soils on glacial sediments.

Hudson Valley soils go from level lake plains (fifty feet above sea level) to very steep capped uplands (eight hundred feet above sea level); slopes range from zero to sixty degrees.

The annual precipitation ranges from thirty to forty-five inches, and the frost-free season ranges from 120 to 180 days. The soil is thick (from twenty to sixty inches), the depth of bedrock is sixty inches and rock fragments, mostly gravel, range from 0 to 25 percent by volume in the mineral and subsurface horizons. There's lots of flavor in our rich, ancient Hudson River Valley region soil—but not all of the tasting notes are universal palate-pleasers in our demanding foodways.

According to the USDA, the Hudson Valley soil "consists of very deep, moderately well drained soils formed in clayey and silty lacustrine sediments. They are nearly level through very steep soils on convex lake plains, on rolling through hilly moraines and on dissected lower valley side slopes. Saturated hydraulic conductivity is moderately high or high in the mineral surface and subsurface layers and low through moderately high in the lower part of the subsoil and substratum. Slope ranges from 0 through 60 percent. Mean annual temperature is 49 degrees F. and mean annual precipitation is 39 inches."

We love learning about how lacustrine sediments and hydraulic conductivity affect our tipple as much as the next soil geek, really. One of our favorite activities around the historic Astor family 220-acre farm known as Empire Farm and home to the FarmOn! Foundation is to gaze out at the fields and surrounding hills and think about the millions of years of geologic activity and thousands upon thousands of years of human history that have led us to grow the perfect lacinato kale and acres and acres of sweet heritage native American heirloom corn and how the soil under our feet that perfectly suits Columbia County for organic agriculture production of heirloom vegetables, fruits and berries and spry free-range chickens running through it all because you are what you—and they—eat and drink. OK, so maybe "one of our favorite activities" is overstating the case, but it does come up, especially on those early fall and late spring Friday afternoons when the light burnishes the fields just so—they really do look like amber waves of grain—and the world seems right and ripe for the magic hour picking.

And when it does and work is over, sometimes we hit one of the local wine trails to experience that magic in sippable form. Drinking wine literally among the vines and fields of the Hudson Valley is one of our favorite ways to celebrate the diverse bounty that our little patch of earth affords us here in our beloved Hudson River Valley. On our many meanderings, we've discovered new favorite wines that aren't even made from grapes. Blasphemy? Not so fast.

Lucky for us, many Hudson Valley winemakers are turning to other fruits to make beverages from their labor—like hard cider and perry, made from apples and pears, respectively. Spirits are also made from fruit. And frequent collaborations among winemakers, distillers and brewers have been kicked into overdrive in recent years, producing small, seasonal batches of Hudson Valley–grown alcoholic beverages that often gloriously blur the lines of beverage classification.

They're simpler and easier (and sometimes more eco-friendly) to grow, and with a little know-how and patience, they can be transformed into drinkable versions of the land from which they sprout.

From a purely aesthetic standpoint, our fruit wines and their ilk are often seen as superior to our grape wines, but like some of the more unfamiliar hybrid and grape varietals we've discussed,

Hillrock solara aged bourbon in private barrels. *Courtesy of FarmOnFoundation.org.*

non-grape fruit wines are a tough sell. They're viewed as wines that haven't graduated to the adult table, for beginners, winos or those of the woods.

But even if you don't have a pair of muck boots or a pair of non-ironic overalls in your closet, your urbanity and sophistication can remain intact while sipping apple wine or cassis. Promise.

Also, it would be difficult to find a more perfect distillation of the region's history and terroir than apple wine (and that's why we're here, right?). The Hudson Valley is, of course, the birthplace of American wine, and the Empire State is synonymous with apples. It is the second-largest producer of apples in America, after all.

"People think of fruit wine as an evil invention," Sue Goold Miller, proprietor of Brookview Station Winery in Castleton, noted wryly. "But in the fifth century, everyone wanted them because they were considered a luxury staple in France of all places. People are grape snobs—and they're missing out. At our tasting room, people are often shocked to find out some of the wines they tasted are from apples, because they're so dry, not cloying at all."

Fruit wines, when properly produced, are complex, aromatic and deliciously refreshing. And yes, they resemble traditional grape wines more than the soda pop–style wine cooler most people picture when uttering the phrase "fruit wine."

Brookview, one of the most beloved fruit wine producers in the valley, makes the popular Whistle-Stop White (a semi-dry wine made from local apples), Oh What a Pear (a semi-dry white made from crushed and fermented local pears), the gloriously aromatic Strawberry Sunrise (whole strawberries are used in the fermentation of the wine) and Conductor's Cassis (a decadent cordial made from Hudson Valley black currants in the traditional French style).

Sue credits the wine's success directly to her forebears and the land itself. The winery was established in 2006, the first winery in Rensselaer County. But its roots go deeper. Brookview is part of Goold Orchards, which was established in 1910 by James and Bertha Goold, her grandparents. James, a Cornell University grad, eagerly applied all of his hard-won book learning along with his innate country wisdom to plant the first seeds of an orchard and farm that would support and feed countless mouths in the generations to come.

"We have glorious soil," Sue says. "If we could have a gravel bank, we'd be millionaires! It's this gorgeous loam, and my grandfather understood how well orchards would grow here. We are on top of the second-largest aquifer in New York State. And our orchards are between the Catskills and Helderberg Mountains, so the sweeping view isn't bad either!"

When Sue and her husband, Edward Miller, began making wine, they realized that the best way to celebrate the Hudson Valley, their heritage and the products of the land was by focusing on non-grape varietals.

"We love producing wine that surprises—in a good way—everyone, from fruit grown right here at our feet," Sue explains.

Brookview is a founding member of the Hudson-Berkshire Beverage Trail, which is often hailed as one of the country's most eclectic trails, featuring wineries, distilleries, microbreweries and cideries. The trail, which meanders through New York and Massachusetts, is also dotted with farms, artisanal bakeries, gourmet farm-to-table fare and, yes, plenty of locals too.

While strawberry, apple, pear and raspberry wine provide an undeniably delicious and distinctively Hudson Valley experience and are perfect for sipping in the season when they're harvested, it would take a lot to make them as trendy again as they were in fifth-century France.

Sue Goold Miller and Ed Miller toast to a delicious harvest. *Courtesy of Brookview Station Winery.*

Cassis and distilled fruit spirits are a different story, though. Cassis, aka crème de cassis, is a dark, rich, sweet red distillation of black currants. It is a specialty of Burgundy and frequently used in sophisticated cocktails, as an after-dinner liqueur or Kir Royal with champagne as an aperitif. Here, locals pour it over ice cream. Adair Vineyards, Brookview, Clinton Vineyards, Glorie Farm Winery, Hudson-Chatham Winery, Tousey Winery, Tuthilltown Spirits and Warwick Valley Winery all produce a cassis made from local fruit with multiuse promotion.

While the Hudson Valley's production of cassis will likely never rival France's (roughly sixteen million liters per year), the production of currants here is seeing a significant revival, which is rewarding to see. A century ago, New York State was the country's top producer of red currants, but blight wiped out much of the acreage. In 1911, the cultivation of black currants was made illegal due to an erroneous belief that they were spreading a fungal disease that endangered pine, according to J. Stephen Casscles, author and wine expert.

In 2003, the ban on black currants was finally lifted, and now dozens of farms in the Hudson Valley and throughout the state are producing the fruit, often for cassis. As economic pressure on farmers from developers and competition with big ag increases, these producers are increasingly turning to the bottle to improve their bottom line.

Harvest Spirits Farm Distillery is another example of a family of farmers who looked beyond the field. Golden Harvest Farms was founded in 1957 in Valatie, New York, by Dan and Madeline Zink, who purchased the old orchard from some of President Van Buren's descendants.

By 1974, when the next generation took over, Alan and Jayne and their five boys, the farm had modernized and expanded to grow fifteen varietals of apples on two one-hundred-acre plots. Fresh cider, apples and home-baked goods kept them fed. But by 2007, Derek Grout (one of the five boys) convinced his dad to turn a cold storage room into a distillery. He wanted to make apple vodka, called Core, from 100 percent farm-grown apples.

In 2008, the first batch was available, and while vodka famously doesn't have a taste, his has a perceptible aroma and a clean mouthfeel that instantly hooked consumers and critics alike—and the packaging was innovative and beautiful.

Harvest's Cornelius Applejack, with the flavor of bourbon rounded out by sweet-tart apples, is their most beloved product, though their brandies, fruit vodkas and eaux de vies are popular too. The applejack is aged for two years in Kentucky bourbon casks, resembles a whiskey more than a brandy

Derek Grout pouring his Core vodka at the HOOT! *Courtesy of FarmOnFoundation.org.*

and is gluten-free for whiskey-loving foes of grain.

The Suarez Family Brewery is a mom-and-pop production specializing in ales of mixed fermentation, unfiltered lagers and other "crispy little beers." Owned and operated by the Suarez family, the brewery will soon open a tasting room in Livingston, New York. This and other new businesses keep us keen on new ideas and local innovators to heighten flavor with technique and savvy.

But our favorite way to enjoy farm-fresh wine is making it ourselves. Hey, we are local. The Saratoga Zymurgist offers a home winemaking class, giving aspiring winemakers a chance to learn the ropes. Many are surprised to discover how fun, accessible and delicious it can be. According to owner and winemaking teacher Reed Antis, "You can make wine from anything."

It sounded good until he presented us with an example of his thesis: an absurdly bright orange tincture, made from garden-grown carrots and aged for one year. Yikes. But the first dubious sip turned into a delighted gulp and then a few more.

Turns out vegetable wine is pretty good. So what's the secret?

"Grapes have tannins, which give wine its body and fullness," Reed explained. "Most other fruits don't, although some cider-making apples do. So while we love to make country wine and mead using all local fruits, herbs and honey, to make it truly delicious, we sprinkle in tannins in a powdered form."

The tannin powder, plus Reed's other tools of the home-wine trade—pectin, yeast, sweetness, acid, yeast nutrient, time—transform your healthy smoothie into a sophisticated, balanced, yet buttery elixir. And it's bright orange—a more perfect tipple for Halloween does not exist.

Mary, Reed's wife, doesn't like wine. But she does weigh in on everything Zym-related, telling us, "Grapes are boring. You're not really having fun until you throw in something from your backyard."

We couldn't agree more.

Reed's Recipe for Apple Pie Mead

1 gallon (12 pounds) honey
2½ gallons water
3 cinnamon sticks
5 cloves
2 nutmeg buttons, grated
Yeast energizer
4 tablespoons acid blend
Dry mead yeast
2 gallons unfiltered (pasteurized) apple cider

Boil honey in 2½ gallons water for 30 minutes; skim scum as it rises. Add all spices and yeast energizer in final 5 minutes; cover and let steep for 15 minutes. Test for acid and add acid blend as desired. Add a pinch of dry mead yeast. Rack in 2 weeks, again in another 4 weeks, again in another 4 weeks. (Don't know how to rack wine? Wikihow and YouTube have great guides.) Bottle when crystal clear.

NB: If all of this sounds too complicated to do at home, just give Reed a ring at Saratoga Zymurgist. He holds regular home winemaking courses for beginners and more advanced students that demystify the process.

Sometimes, locally made (sometimes backyard hootch) non-grape wine is the best way to taste the most elevated and elegant distillation of the Hudson Valley's land, history and people. Now you know. Get your FarmOn!

7

THE TASTEMAKERS

The DIY ethos is ingrained in Hudson Valley folks' DNA. From moms with the school board on speed dial to businesses large and small, the philosophy is, if you want it and it doesn't exist, create it yourself. See a problem? Fix it.

The foundation for the wine industry in the Hudson Valley was built, a little at a time, by a lot of people who took it upon themselves to patch up cracks in the cement. Here it is, 2017, ranking third in the country for wine production, winning accolades from around the world for our wines. But what was our journey here, and where will we end up?

Between Prohibition (1920–1933) and, depending on who you ask, but probably sometime in the early 2000s, the wine industry in the Hudson Valley was a national joke—but definitely not one we were laughing at.

Until 1976, when the Farm Winery Act was passed, the state instituted rules and restrictions that made small-scale vineyards almost an impossibility. The Farm Winery Act allowed wineries to operate small-scale vineyards and sell directly to customers. Before the legislation was passed, there were fewer than two licensed wineries in the state. Now there are more than three hundred. The same explosive growth is true for breweries and spirits producers as well.

These days, going into a bar or restaurant and finding a locally made libation is simple—Millbrook Winery's Cabernet Franc, Keegan's Mother's Milk and Tuthilltown's Whiskey are just the automatics. Forward-thinking restaurants generally have at least a dozen to choose from. Deciding *which* local wine, spirit or beer to drink is the tough part. That wasn't always the case.

Historically, the government's role in legislation involving booze has been designed to restrict, rather than encourage, the consumption of alcohol. But under the leadership of Governor Andrew Cuomo, New York's lawmakers have embraced artisans and farmers in the business of creating New York–made wine, beer, cider and alcohol.

Since 2011, Governor Cuomo has been making it easier for small-scale wine, beer and spirit makers to create scalable business models from scratch. New York has created new farm-based manufacturing licenses and launched a near $60 million statewide promo campaign that has made the state home to more than nine hundred breweries, distilleries and cideries. The sweeping actions have simplified regulations and cut through red tape, which has resulted in an unprecedented three-fold increase in licensed wineries, breweries, distilleries and cideries across the state becoming an economic engine.

The number of farm wineries has grown an astounding 60 percent to about 315 today from 195 in 2010. In September 2016, Governor Cuomo instituted a law that authorizes the sale of wine in growlers and allows wineries to permit customers to take home partially finished bottles of wine. The same law also loosened so-called Sunday sales, put in place by God-fearing (or maybe just fun-fearing?) people some eighty years ago. So yes, that does mean everyone can get their brunch wine on at 10:00 a.m. instead of noon on Sundays.

Creating windows of opportunities for small boutique businesses across the state is having a real impact on the lives of New Yorkers and those who visit the Hudson Valley—and not just because they can order a locally made wine spritzer with their farm-fresh eggs and bacon at 10:30 a.m.

Since 2015, 177 new manufacturing licenses have been issued, and if you count distribution and retail, producers make a $27 billion economic impact that supports tens of thousands of jobs statewide.

The almost eerily successful campaign to create jobs and revive depressed rural economies around the state (though of course, much still needs to be done) is a fantastic example of a lot of squeaky wheels making a little progress on separate projects at the same time.

It just happened that the governor and his team had the foresight and the cooperation of other legislators to put the squeaky wheels together and provide the money to fuel the happy little bar cart we didn't know we wanted until it pulled in.

The New York native Concord grape, beloved when spread on toast in the form of jam, is less prized in the glass for its foxy flavors. Reprinted with permission from *Grapes of the Hudson Valley and Other Cool Climate Regions of the United States and Canada* by J. Stephen Casscles. *Courtesy of Flint Mine Press.*

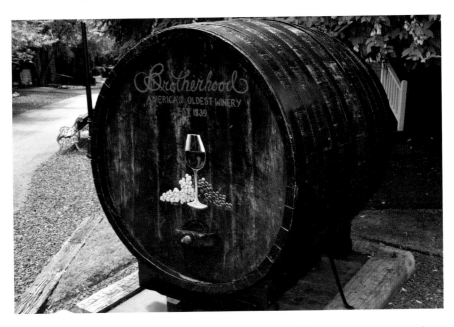

The gorgeous grounds and fabulous history of Brotherhood Winery merit a trip as much as the winery's signature Hudson Valley wines do. *Courtesy of Brotherhood Winery.*

Wineries up and down the Hudson Valley have been producing farm-to-bottle wines for generations. *Courtesy of the Hudson-Berkshire Beverage Trail.*

Cooking over open fire with Staub at Alice Waters wine dinner at Empire Farm. *Courtesy of FarmOnFoundation. org.*

Chef Terrance Brennan's inspiration for onion soup. *Courtesy of Roundhouse Beacon.*

Left: Fall foliage at Empire Farm. *Courtesy of Tara Boyles.*

Below: Hudson Valley local libations feature fruit wines, local spirits and ciders. *Courtesy of Roundhouse Beacon.*

Above: Sunrise melting frost in the Hudson Valley. *Courtesy of Tara Boyles.*

Left: Chef Jonathan Wright's oysters and pâté en croûte make perfect local wine pairings. *Courtesy of Tessa Edick.*

Aging wine takes on new meaning at America's oldest winery. *Courtesy of Brotherhood Winery.*

Taste NY at Grand Central window. *New York State.*

Left: Under a cerulean blue sky, the green just seems to stretch on forever. *Courtesy of the Hudson-Berkshire Beverage Trail.*

Right: Riesling originated in the Rhine region of Germany but grows beautifully here, delivering a perfumed bouquet and refreshingly fruity high-acid flavor. Reprinted with permission from *Grapes of the Hudson Valley and Other Cool Climate Regions of the United States and Canada* by J. Stephen Casscles. *Courtesy of Flint Mine Press.*

Autumn in the vineyards of the Hudson Valley is its own special delight. *Courtesy of Millbrook Winery.*

A majestic view awaits at Millbrook Winery. *Courtesy of Millbrook Winery.*

Decisions, decisions. *Courtesy of Millbrook Winery.*

Vineyard horizon. *New York State.*

Local food and wine at the historic Bartlett House Bakery and Café in Ghent, New York. *Courtesy of Bartlett House.*

Left: Chef Giovanni Scappin of Rhinebeck, New York. *Courtesy of Market Street.*

Right: Chef Tom Kacherski of Crew Restaurant, Poughkeepsie, New York. *Courtesy of Tom Kacherski.*

Village Tea Room in New Paltz, New York, is committed to local food and wine. *Courtesy of Keith Ferris.*

The blossom that begins wine production in the Hudson Valley, just starting on its long journey to the bottle. *Courtesy of the Wine and Grape Foundation.*

Rest and renewal is key to good wine in the Hudson Valley. *Courtesy of Trevor Valley Farm.*

Local food and wine at Terrapin Restaurant in the Hudson Valley. *Courtesy of Chef Josh Kroner.*

Picking and pressing are the best days to volunteer for winemaking in the Hudson Valley. *Courtesy of Trevor Valley Farm.*

Harvesting the fruit of terroir in the Hudson Valley. *Courtesy of the Wine and Grape Foundation.*

A view of the Hudson Valley from above. Look at all of that gorgeous green. *Courtesy of the Wine and Grape Foundation.*

Fog over Trevor Valley Farm Vineyard. *Courtesy of Michael Rietbrock and Susan Pearson.*

Hudson Valley farm through the fog. *Courtesy of Stephen Mack.*

A chicken in the back of a truck with produce. *Courtesy of FarmOnFoundation.org.*

Pat Hooker, currently the deputy secretary for agriculture and markets and the state liquor authority and previously the director of agribusiness development for the Empire State Development Corporation, knows better than anyone how essential certain individuals and organizations have been in helping to inspire and shape the sweeping vision of the legislation around local libations.

"Producers and entrepreneurs are critical to the process," Hooker explains. "Democracy and government don't work unless you have active participants on both sides of the aisle. Reflecting back to when the governor started his first term, it's incredibly complicated to think about how it all started, but he prioritized growing the upstate economy from the start, he wanted to increase tourism and he wanted to make the government more efficient."

Because of the activist nature of some producers, Governor Cuomo became aware of the listless state of the wine, beer and alcohol industry, and evidently, he became convinced that simplifying this one sector in a handful of straightforward ways (promotion, easing restrictions, eliminating red tape) would drive tourism, improve the economy and create opportunities for small businesses.

One entrepreneur Hooker mentions again and again (as does almost every other insider involved in any way, shape and form in the transformation of the New York adult beverage sector) is Ralph Erenzo.

Erenzo quickly emerged as an unlikely but highly effective industry transformer who had the power to captivate legislators, engage local farmers and attract the kind of attention and interest from members of the press that inevitably results in glowing profiles and hordes of thirsty visitors.

In 2001, Ralph purchased property in Gardiner to create a climbers' ranch, where Shawangunk hikers liked to hang out. Disapproving locals moved to shut down his plan. With a costly court battle and a major real estate purchase in his rearview mirror, Erenzo, who previously provided technical services to corporate and media clients, made a weird, happy discovery.

Ferrier Barn with Taste NY signs at Empire Farm. *Courtesy of FarmOnFoundation.org.*

In 2002, a law appeared on the books that slashed the cost of licensing a micro-distillery making up to thirty-five thousand gallons of aged grain spirits to $1,450 from more than $50,000, he tells *Hudson Valley Wine* magazine. Big difference.

Ralph, eager to recoup some of his losses and create something that reflected the beauty of the Gunks and the surrounding land, made a snap decision to embark on a journey that not only enriched him personally but also improved the lives and futures of thousands of future wine and spirits makers.

Around the time he discovered the bargain-basement distillery licensing deal, he met Brian Lee, and the two hit it off over a conversation about the old Tuthilltown Gristmill on Erenzo's land. (The gristmill has been a landmark since it was built in 1788 and is listed in the National Register of Historic Places. It used water power to render local grains to flour.) He and Lee, who worked as a technical designer for a company building broadcast television facilities, partnered together, pledging to use booze as a vehicle to showcase the terroir of the Hudson Valley. The gristmill was back in business—this time as a micro-distillery.

Every spirit Tuthilltown produces is made from grain harvested by farmers less than ten miles away or apples grown at orchards just five miles away. They taste of the land, the river, those gorgeous Gunks.

As Erenzo explained in an interview for *Hudson Valley Wine* magazine, "In the Hudson Valley, spirit-making is an agricultural craft, not an industrial product." "We started the process in 2003 and managed to get the Farm Distillery License Act passed in 2007," Erenzo recalled. "We had three governors in those four years, and we had to amend it twice before it was passed. By the time everything was said and done, we ensured that once distillers acquired a Farm Distillery License, they could officially possess farm status. That's important because farm status in New York comes with various rights, privileges and latitude."

Privileges like lowering fees and operating a tasting room on-site are essential for boot-strapping booze pioneers. Caveats in the law ensured that the Hudson Valley would remain a bucolic paradise, even as (small-scale) industry moved in. Makers were required to follow strict environmental standards and use, you know, actual farm products.

In 2012, Cuomo convened the first New York Wine, Beer and Spirits Summit in Albany, with makers and farmers coming together to exchange notes and, yes, bitch. Afterward, Cuomo pledged $5 million on marketing to promote local libations, which included coordinating regional restaurant weeks that highlight New York–made tipples and ensuring that local beverages are sold at New York Racing Association tracks.

Why are we talking about Tuthilltown in a book about wine? Because Erenzo, more than anyone else, ensured the passage of the Farm Distillery License Act in 2007, which drastically reduced fees for would-be producers and simplified the process. The only caveat (some view it as a catch, others as an added bonus) is that the vast majority of their product had to be sourced from New York farms, a brilliant way to help ensure the financial success of the faltering rural economy and help lift up the entire region—grape growers and winemakers included.

The success of the distillery program also highlighted what producers have been trying to tell Albany for years: a craft alcohol, wine and beer industry is good for farmers, tourism and the local economy. A cavalcade of acts followed, notably the Craft New York Act, which committed $3 million to the promotion of New York wine, beer and spirits and eliminated some of the more stringent tasting room policies.

Without visionaries like Erenzo and effective legislators who were audacious enough to actually change the status quo, bars and liquor stores in New York would be boring bastions of California Chardonnay and French Merlot. Other figures, while having significantly less name recognition, have arguably had just as much, if not more, influence on the state of New York's wine industry.

You won't find any glowing profiles of them in glossies, and they're clearly more comfortable behind the scenes than in front of flashing cameras. Through their glossy *Hudson Valley Wine* magazine and the Flint Mine printing press, Robert Bedford and Linda Pierro have been essentially shaping the public's perceptions of the history, current state and potential future direction of wine in New York.

Established in 2008, the magazine is the leading authority on the region's wine, beer and spirits through profiles of leading producers, features exploring trends in the industry and travel tips and maps. It has become a must-get for tourists and locals who want to know about the coolest new startup vineyards and the pros and cons of pairing one esoteric hybrid grape with salmon over another. Additional, roughly twenty thousand copies are distributed free of charge twice a year, and it appears in its entirety online sans paywall.

Want to know what to expect when you open a bottle of Chambourcin? Or which wineries are employing the most cutting-edge green technology? Want ideas on where to stop on a wine tour and why? They've got you covered.

Pierro and Bedford, who are partners in life and business, inherited their roles as tastemakers by happy accident.

"We started working together thirty years ago at design studios in Manhattan," Pierro recalled. "Our careers have been very different. He was producing events, and I was doing design. We always had a passion for wine and often structured our vacations around traveling to vineyards that interested us."

Pierro, like many converts from Manhattan to the Hudson Valley, dipped her toe in business initially. She began producing marketing materials and

Wine bottles. *New York State*.

brochures for tourism agencies in the Hudson Valley, and around the same time, she and Bedford heard a report on the radio about how global climate change was going to affect the wine industry in New York.

"It was the early 2000s, and I had just completed a wine map of the region for a tourism board when I heard that Staten Island might become a good place for vineyards if the warming trend continues," Linda explained. "The report talked about how the vineyards in the Hudson Valley would be cast aside. The birthplace of wine in America! I couldn't believe it."

Pierro and Bedford's fascination with wine and the manner in which it is grown, promoted and consumed in the region extended far beyond the usual armchair interest. Between his background as an archivist, curator and historian and hers in tourism and promotion, they began sketching out plans for a publication that would allow them to flex their creative muscles and pool their collective talents and interest into a business that would not only support them financially but also boost an entire region.

They approached producers, tourist boards and local movers and shakers and found that there was a dire need for a unified, confident voice to speak for the region.

"The region needed a nonpartisan advocate who wasn't tied to one specific area of the valley and wasn't trying to discredit one producer in favor of another," she said. By 2007, they were hard at work on the first issue, and while funding was, as she puts it, "by the seat of [their] pants," it trickled in, through ads by producers and through the support of wine trails and local businesses.

From the get-go, their goal has been to draw visitors to the under-appreciated region and educate them on the unique charms that can be found in a Hudson Valley wine.

"It's in Manhattan's backyard, so people come here to go camping and skiing and hiking, but the vineyards were often overlooked," Linda said. "We have always tried to get other industries involved in the promotion—art galleries, festivals—because it's in everyone's interest to show people how much there is to do right here. We also really wanted people to understand that their options at the liquor store don't just have to be a California Chardonnay or a French Bordeaux. Yes, they're wonderful, but there are so many other exciting varietals to be explored, right here in their backyard!"

One of the trademark rallying calls of all regional food movements has become drink or eat local first. Pierro and Bedford caught—and spread—the buzz before it was hip, and it appears that consumers are finally starting to listen. Especially millennials.

In 2015, people in their twenties and thirties guzzled 159.6 million cases of wine, 42 percent of all wine consumed in the United States. And unlike the drinkers of yore, these whippersnappers weren't looking to France or Italy for their grapes. They want organic or sustainably produced bottles (51 percent according to a Creative Feed study) from "real" producers who they connect with either in person, via social media or through apps like Vivino and Delectable, which allow users to share wine reviews instantly and research production and growing methods in a just a few lazy (sometimes hazy) swipes.

The magazine was a runaway success with locals, tourists and producers, and in 2009, the couple launched their book publishing arm: the Flint Mine Press. Bob's *The Story of Brotherhood, America's Oldest Winery*, was published in 2014, and several other books, including one on mushrooms by Dom Laudato, *Mushrooming on Long Island: Selected Memoirs of an Obsessed Mycophile*, have preceded and followed.

Their message—that not just noble grapes grown on the Gold Coast or in central Europe are worth drinking—isn't just resonating with millennials. It seems that the same fancy glossies that held their noses at Hudson Valley wines and the restaurants in Manhattan that refused to serve them are finally coming around too. (They'd lose readers and customers if they didn't.)

"A few years ago, most people hadn't heard of Baco Noir," Pierro said. "And even if they still haven't yet, we've found once we break it down for them in a column with a bit of history, tasting notes and include a recipe with it, they are much more likely to try it and appreciate it. There's been a real change across the country in the way people look at their sources of food and drink. They understand that the little everyday choices they make have an impact not just on them, but their neighborhood, their region, their state, their community."

It's a lot of little. A lot of little changes snowball, roll into boulders, careen forward and build into an avalanche.

While Erenzo could speak truth to power (and get heard), and Pierro and Bedford could recognize a treasure in danger of desecration, Cornell University has, for more than a century, literally helped plant the seeds in our region's vineyards. Unlike some of the other more renegade individuals who have added zest and complexity to the cocktail of craft production in New York, Cornell University's role has been anything but accidental.

Since 1906, Cornell has been breeding grapes and has released more than fifty juice, table and wine grape varieties adapted to cool climates and ideal for growing in the Hudson Valley. Scientists and researchers work with

A lovely, food-friendly wine, Baco Noir's dark berry flavors serve as a counterpoint to dark poultry and smoky game meats. *Courtesy of the Hudson-Berkshire Beverage Trail.*

growers to evaluate current and potential vineyard sites based on geography, climate and data they run on soil samples. The lab also analyzes wine samples to flag problems.

Sustainability has become a focus as well, and Cornell has developed programs to work with producers on organic growing programs that will still produce beautiful, pest-free vines without hurting their bottom line.

"Cornell and the Agricultural Experiment Station have been working for more than 100 years to combat grape disease and improve the way grapes are grown and harvested," Chris Gerling, an extension associate and manager of the Vinification Brewing Laboratory at Cornell, explained. "In New York State specifically, we have helped growers as the interest in growing wine grapes as opposed to juice grapes has increased. There are certain diseases and pests that are prevalent here that the hybrid grapes we've developed can resist."

Hybrid grapes are the result of two or more *Vitis* species. In the early 1900s, breeding programs were used to combat the notorious phylloxera pest, a louse responsible for the destruction of European vineyards. By grafting European varieties to North American rootstock, the vines could resist the pest.

The zeal for hybrids in Europe had an unexpected consequence in regions like New York with cooler temperatures, more humidity and shorter seasons than generally considered ideal. Often, hybrid crosses between grapes native to New York and grapes native to Europe produced hardier grapes that flourish in the tough Hudson Valley climate.

"We want the same thing the grower wants," Chris said. "We want to produce a grape that can develop into a wine with characteristics that meet or exceed what is currently available and has better disease resistance and

119

Good enough to eat, but even better fermented, aged and sipped. *Courtesy of the Hudson-Berkshire Beverage Trail.*

hardiness. We don't want the farmers to have to use a lot of spray to ward off pests, and you have to do that out here with the pure European varieties. One exception is Cabernet Franc. I see a lot of promise for that in the Hudson Valley. Another is Chardonnay and Reisling. Millbrook has put in a fair amount, and it has great potential."

The members of the Hudson Valley Cabernet Franc Coalition would agree.

Of the hybrids, Chris, like many others, sang the praises of Baco Noir and Traminette, which mimics Gewürztraminer but is more suitable for the climate.

"So many of us buy milk, cheese, produce and meat from the farmers' market," Pierro said. "It's fresher, more nutritious and we know it supports our community. Why wouldn't we buy our local wine made from local grapes?"

For all of the same reasons we must not buy asparagus from Mexico in January and opt for butternut squash instead, the move to pass that Bordeaux over for that Baco Noir, thanks to people like Erenzo, Pierro and Bedford, is on. And thanks to Cornell University and, of all things, the New York State government and its Taste NY initiative, our bar car is about to pick up a lot more passengers.

8

ENSURING THE FUTURE

*A*dvertising seems like a dirty concept, one fraught with calculation, with a whiff of deception—especially for earnest, smart, well-meaning farm-to-bottlers allergic to false narratives and trickery, immersed in authenticity and transparent practices.

But if we've learned anything in the past ten years of dramatic political, economic and cultural change, we have learned that success and failure for individuals and companies are tightly associated with promotion.

Love 'em or hate 'em, think of Uber, Target, Bud Light. Think of the carefully calibrated spin around the Kardashians, Apple, Harley Davidson, Tiffany & Co. Just the names conjure up a whole host of images and associations that we are intrinsically attracted to and occasionally repelled by, depending on how we define our true selves and the manner in which the ideals they project align with (or fail to) our own values.

The Hudson Valley is branded by history, heritage and light. The founders of our country took care of that. Whether it is our bracing political, military or creative history; the region's physical beauty; or its wealth of cultural offerings, its current cache as a bohemian chic retreat for urbane sophisticates is calling, and on some level, the Hudson Valley is universally attractive for most.

On the other hand, Hudson Valley wine has been a work in progress. Linda Pierro and Bob Bedford helped lay the groundwork with their publication *Hudson Valley Wine* magazine. But their latest project, the Hudson Valley Cabernet Franc Coalition, has perfectly captured the art and science of

Be a local food hero. *Village Tea Room, New Paltz, New York.*

branding magic that, while impossible to define, is instantly recognizable and has transformative powers for the people behind it.

Like many excellent plans, it was hatched with a friend over a fabulous glass of wine.

"It was a serendipitous culmination of several things," Linda recalled. "We were at a festival a few years ago, and I was going from table to table tasting these incredible Cab Francs. Benmarl had just received a rave review in *Wine Spectator* for their Cab Franc. I stopped by Doug Glorie's booth at Glorie Winery to try his Cab Franc, and we got to talking about the amazing progress the grape had made in the region."

Cab Franc is a French grape, striking in its almost pitch-black color. It is renowned not only for its role in Right Bank Bordeaux but also Loire Valley wines. It fizzes with bright raspberry flavor, a distinctive cherry scent and a zesty, spicy finish. When grown in suitable soil, it is forthright, juicy, well rounded and balanced. Cab Franc can impart unpleasant vegetal green pepper flavors when the growing conditions aren't ideal.

Clearly, many in the Hudson Valley had already found ways to overcome the grape's handicaps. *Wine Enthusiast* rated Millbrook Vineyard Winery's Millbrook 2013 Special Reserve Cabernet Franc ninety-one, the 2015 Proprietor's Special Reserve Tocai Fruilano a ninety and the 2014 Cabernet Franc a ninety. *WE* rated Benmarl Winery's Benmarl 2012 Ridge Road Estate Cabernet Franc ninety and Whitecliff Vineyard's Whitecliff 2013 Cabernet Franc ninety points.

For Benmarl, Cabernet Franc has been the muse that helped it rewrite its story. The Spaccarelli family bought Benmarl in 2006 from the Miller family. When the Spaccarellis first arrived, there was only one estate wine on tap and only two and a half highly productive vineyard acres, Matt Spaccarelli of Benmarl explained. When they bought the winery, Kristop Brown was bumped up from assistant winemaker to winemaker, and Matt trained under him. The duo remain close, bouncing ideas off of each other. When Kristop moved on, Matt took over.

Under Kristop and then Matt's guidance, Benmarl scaled up sustainably.

The winery is committed to making small-batch wines that capture the essence of each vineyard and using integrated pest management. (Instead of spraying pesticides, the winery has sheep and lambs graze the vineyard. Effective, eco-conscious and picturesque.)

In a review that launched the winery onto restaurant wine lists and into liquor cabinets across the country, *Wine Enthusiast* characterized Benmarl's 2012 Ridge Road Estate Cabernet Franc thusly: "Ripe red-cherry and blossom aromas are accented with char and toast on this aromatic, spirited Cabernet Franc. The palate is brisk, with fresh black-cherry and plum flavors wrapped in fine-grained tannins and a savory herbal edge."

In 2013, Matt founded Fjord Vineyards, also in Marlboro, with Casey Erdmann. At Benmarl, Matt had a lot of creative freedom, but at Fjord, his winemaking is even more aggressively experimental and cutting-edge. The audacity is paying off: Fjord won winery of the year in the 2016 Hudson Valley Wine Competition. Fjord is producing the Hudson Valley's only estate-planted Albarino, Riesling, Sauvignon Blanc, Chardonnay, Merlot and, of course, Cabernet Franc.

The fact that a winery that has declared itself as experimental is planting so much vinifera underlines the assertion that Linda, Bob, Doug and so many others are making: a rarefied, traditional, familiar grape can provide the perfect basis for a tasteful revolution.

Cab Franc is naturally a hardy vinifera that makes it ideal for the Hudson Valley (which has similar climactic conditions as Loire, France, where it is also the signature varietal). The grape is also the parent of Cabernet Sauvignon and Merlot, two of the most beloved grapes of all time.

Linda, Bob, Doug and MaryEllen Glorie were encouraged by the promise Cab Franc had shown and became convinced that not only could its drawbacks be managed with some tweaking but also by making it the region's signature grape, the region would be able to increase the quality of its wines overall and brand itself more effectively.

"In October of 2015, after months of reaching out to other growers, producers and researchers, we started to put the plan in motion," Linda recalled. "At that time, [there] were about twelve people growing Cab Franc and twelve people making it, a huge percentage of the makers in the valley. But there wasn't a tremendous amount of acreage devoted to it."

Still, the wineries that were producing Cab Franc were getting excellent results, a fact that is bolstered by critical acclaim and sales.

"In tasting rooms, people love the hybrids and unfamiliar varietals," Linda said. "But people do gravitate toward vinifera elsewhere."

She has an excellent point. People in tasting rooms are a captive audience. They come to the winery with an open mind and palate. Gazing out a window and seeing a vineyard with plump, juicy grapes ripening under the sun with a fantastic spread of local cheese on a board in front of them, chatting with the person who made the wine in the glass they're sipping from, learning the story of how the wine is made and who makes it, relaxing with a lover or friend—it's an undeniably magical experience.

Those are the moments—breaking bread, exploring new flavors in a relaxing setting with someone we love, when obligations and stress are momentarily tabled—that we all remember forever; they are the essence of the human experience. Licking a stray drop of garnet off of our smiling lips, tipping back that last luscious sip, the last thing we're thinking about is whether we prefer this funky hybrid to the Merlot we typically gravitate toward at home.

At a liquor store or restaurant though, it's a different story. Then we want something familiar; we don't want to puzzle over our choice like it's a multiple-choice question on the SAT.

Even Stephen Osborn, founder of natural winery Stoutridge and unabashed advocate of unusual grapes, is behind the Cab Franc movement, for all of the reasons Linda cited.

"I love the Cab Franc movement," he says. "We're not personally growing it right now, because everyone else is, but I think the manner in which its flavors are expressed in Hudson Valley soil is wonderful, and I support any movement that makes Hudson Valley wine dig into its terroir."

The goal is to increase acreage, create a unified identity for the region and coordinate with scientists and researchers on which varietals of Cab

"Wine is a living liquid containing no preservatives. Its life cycle comprises youth, maturity, old age and death. When not treated with reasonable respect it will sicken and die." - Julia Child

Julia Child, the queen of food and wine. *Courtesy of FarmOnFoundation.org.*

Franc are most suitable for specific vineyards. The coalition became official in February 2016 and received nonprofit status in July.

"Having a signature grape is going to give the Hudson Valley a unified identity, and that can help drive economic development, focus marketing efforts and encourage tourism," Linda said.

The coalition is new, but it has clearly made a splash.

As of 2016, ten additional acres of Cab Franc were planted for newer and more established producers. Many of the growers and winemakers who are prominently involved in the Hudson Valley Heritage Red and Heritage White wine movement—most notably Michael Migliore—are also involved in the Hudson Valley Cabernet Franc Coalition.

The grande dames of Hudson Valley wine—Millbrook, Whitecliff (Michael Migliore's winery) and Benmarl—are deeply involved, as are Robibero Winery, Nostrano, Brunswick and Milea, among others.

Glorie, Whitecliff, Benmarl and Millbrook have been growing Cab Franc for decades, and they are imparting the knowledge gleaned from good and bad harvests to newer growers in the coalition. Also promising is a discovery Cornell University's Cooperative Extension made that may eliminate any of the dreaded vegetal flavor notes that sometimes arise in Cab Francs grown here.

By planting test patches of Cab Franc and rigorously monitoring and testing the grapes at every stage of growth, researchers at Cornell determined that discouraging the development of a chemical compound called methoxypyrines by pruning a vineyard's canopy early in the season eliminates the undesirable green pepper notes.

Researchers at the independent nonprofit organization Hudson Valley Research Lab in Highland, New York, which is affiliated with Cornell University and Cornell University's Cooperative Extension, are examining which varieties of grapes perform best in the region. They are devoting a one-acre test vineyard to a mix of Cabernet Franc clones so local growers can know which strains of this signature grape do best throughout the region.

Every patch of land is a unique microcosm of weather. A vineyard's exposure to the tempering effects of the Hudson River, its elevation, soil drainage, exposure to the sun and many other factors can determine which Cab Franc clone will flourish. When winemakers are seeking—as they are here—transcendence, every minute detail can make a difference.

As part of the initial Cab Franc marketing push, *Hudson Valley Wine* magazine devoted its summer 2016 issue to the glorious grape. It featured a blind tasting conducted by Steven Kolpan, author and professor of wine

The big squeeze. *Courtesy of the Hudson-Berkshire Beverage Trail.*

studies at the Culinary Institute of America in Hyde Park; wine writer Wendy Crispell; Hudson Valley wine goddess Debbie Gioquindo; and organizer of the Hudson Valley Wine and Spirits Competition Amy Zavatto of about twenty Cab Francs made in the region.

THEIR FAVORITES

ROBIBERO, 2013 CABERNET FRANC. *HVW* said, "The rich, dense, dark fruit here shows the influence of the 2013 vintage with ripe, concentrated notes of blackberry, black plum, raspberry and cocoa."

BENMARL, 2012 CABERNET FRANC RIDGE ROAD ESTATE. *HVW* said, "Deep, rich ruby in color, the nose on the 2012 starts out a little reluctant, but give it a minute and it will reward you with pretty notes of flowers and dried raspberry, with an undercurrent of wild cedar and pomegranate. On the palate, this wine is alive—nervous and energetic with tart, bright fruit and a finish of baking spice and black pepper."

WHITECLIFF VINEYARD, 2012 CABERNET FRANC. *HVW* said, "Its clear, medium-ruby hue belies the rich, ripe red-plum fruit and flowers on the nose. In your mouth, things get even more interesting: this juicy, nicely balanced wine yields notes of ripe plum, blackberry, tea, and a hum of minerality."

WHITECLIFF VINEYARD, 2013 CABERNET FRANC. *HVW* said, "The nice, grippy structure here creates a gorgeous foundation to hold all that pretty fruit on the palate, along with notes of black pepper, tea, and streamlined minerality."

FJORD VINEYARDS, 2014 CABERNET FRANC. *HVW* said, "Spaccarelli teases out bright, bursting notes of summer raspberry, strawberry, spice, and dried, sweet herbs. That alert, zippy quality in the Benmarl label is here, too, but the 2014 has a juicy, charming, lip-smacking personality that makes this wine disappear like a wave in the river."

GLORIE FARM WINERY, 2014 CABERNET FRANC. *HVW* said, "The nose is like a late-spring hike in the Shawangunk Ridge, with notes of white pine, cedar, and a little cocoa. On the palate, this complex Cab Franc offered up blackberry, green peppercorns, licorice, and sweet tannins, with a sticky, mouth-watering finish of mixed-berries and tea."

MILLBROOK, 2013 CABERNET FRANC. *HVW* said, "Rich, ripe, juicy blackberry notes morph into strawberry, raspberry and black pepper on the palate. This is a brawny, rich Franc that, given some well-deserved time in your cellar, will grow into itself and its tight, tangy tannins."

HVW called NOSTRANO VINEYARDS' 2014 ESTATE CABERNET FRANC one to watch: "The winery was established in 2014, so the estate fruit of that labor is just beginning to make its debut. We were pretty excited about the potential we saw in Bozzo's 2014 Cabernet Franc. Although this wine possesses a little bit of the greenness that growers are working to cast out, the bones are here: clean, beautiful, bright fruit that leads to notes of strawberry and tea."

When you think Finger Lakes, you think Riesling. Soon, when you think Hudson Valley wine, you'll think Cab Franc.

9

NAPA VALLEY OF THE EAST?

NEXT STEPS FOR NEW YORK STATE WINES

The Hudson Valley wine industry has never been in a better position to honor its past and ensure its future to be celebrated as the very first wine region in the United States of America.

A confluence of events, including the terroir-driven pioneering grape varietal research at the New York State Agricultural Experiment Station at Cornell, has quite literally taken over our fields with an invested commitment; a wide following of critics and sommeliers who are reaping the harvest of those fields to spread the good word to their followers; and savvy local publishers and tourism gurus, who in turn are drawing in new visitors with innovative strategies and a friendly business climate that encourages a successful wine business to culminate in a bumper crop of opportunities for producers, visitors and residents alike.

According to the Department of Labor, as of 2016, there were 460 wineries in New York. These wineries produced more than 200 million bottles of wine in 2014 (the most recent numbers available) and continue to trend upward.

When veering into seven-digit budget categories, with the state pledging to spend nearly $6 million promoting New York's craft beverage industry, it's tough to conceptualize what that actually means to people on the ground who are just trying to make a living fermenting grape juice and other fruit. But drill down below the numbers and stats; New York has reached out globally with advertising campaigns and a relentless presence at trade shows. Tourists from halfway across the world who would never conceive of taking

Wine harvesting in the Hudson Valley. *Courtesy of Tessa Edick.*

a special trip to the Hudson Valley for wine, cider or spirits are now tagging three-day country jaunts onto their trips to New York City.

"At the very top of the valley, we are three hours away from New York City," Karen Gardy, director of the Hudson-Berkshire Beverage Trail, said. "That's a day trip. And now that international travelers know how much there is to see and taste out here, they're signing up for tours and getting out here. And then, they go home and tell their friends. Over the past five years, I have seen steady growth, and that's thanks to the state's campaign but also our ability as producers to work together and cross-market."

The Hudson-Berkshire Beverage Trail is particularly compelling for visitors because it meanders through two states (New York and Massachusetts) and includes breweries and distilleries, so there's something for everyone and it's accessible for a day trip from Boston or Manhattan.

Cross-promotional strategy, in New York, starts at the state level.

Governor Andrew Cuomo's stealth focus on craft beverages and tourism complement each other, but more importantly, they bring in record revenue for the state and lend fair pay to its makers and the people who live in our communities. Traveler spending reached a record high of $63.1 billion in 2015, generating $102 billion in total business sales, including indirect impacts.

Within those billions, of course, is the burgeoning wine sector. In a study conducted for the New York Wine and Grape Foundation by the Stonebridge Research Group, more than 5.29 million tourists with wine-related visas visited the state in 2012. Most of these folks stopped for meals at local restaurants, spent nights in hotels and made other fun-related expenditures at local shops and businesses, as one does on vacation.

This wine-related spending enriches the local economy. For every 100 new winery jobs created in New York, an additional 121 local jobs are created, according to a study from Cornell University on regional multipliers.

Since the passage of the Farm Winery Act in 1976, the state has steadily made strides forward, increasing the number of wineries in-state twenty-fold and producing wines that can impress even the most refined Frenchman for a fraction of the cost.

To people on the ground, the changes in recent years have been unprecedented, a dream realized.

"Unlike other industries, the wine world is a community," according to Lydia Higginson, former vice president of Dutchess County Tourism. "Winemakers here are often the ones in tasting rooms explaining their process, their inspiration and educating consumers about the grapes they grow and how they express themselves through the terroir. They're also often recommending the wineries down the road to stop at, giving visitors insight into the history of the region and their favorite restaurants. Often, winemakers in the Hudson Valley are welcoming visitors into their homes, so people get a very different experience here than they will anywhere else. And guess what? They tell their friends."

Drawing in visitors from afar who are ready and willing to drink deeply of the Hudson Valley wine, culture, history and farm-fresh food is imperative. But getting local consumers and restaurateurs on board the local drinking train is more important, because the choices they make on a daily basis are important not only to the industry's bottom line but also to the heart and soul of the community it serves.

Neal Rosenthal's heart and soul know wine better than most. Author of *Reflections of a Wine Merchant* and the founder of Mad Rose Group, Rosenthal is a resident of the Hudson Valley and a globally renowned wine merchant. Wine means so much more to him than simply the pleasure of taste. He is dedicated to discovery and terroir, a lover of local food and farms (including his own) but not a dealer for New York wines nor embedded in the wine scene locally. Instead, his wine acumen is focused globally and anchored in Europe, but the concept of terroir guides his expertise and rules his life.

At his lovely home in the Hudson Valley, he retreats from the pressures and cares of his globetrotting career to keep bees and chickens, cook and create immense family meals from locally sourced ingredients with his spouse, Kerry. Rosenthal is also very interested in locally grown fruit for all kinds of wine and believes that our Hudson Valley orchards offer the best bounty regionally to explore, expand and drink fruit beyond the grape.

Hudson Valley landscape. *Courtesy of Stephen Mack.*

His first experience thirty-five years ago in the Hudson Valley wine region was connected to honest, solid, drinkable wines that were enjoyable but not so celebrated. He fondly remembers friends from Benmarl, Cascade Mountain and Clinton Vineyards and recalls their bottles as memorable sips of Hudson Valley terroir. Simply remembering the wines brings him back in time to conversations shared over glasses of wine and good local food.

"When producing pleasant and enjoyable local wines to pair with local food, terroir has to be discussed, because how it expresses itself and how farmers/producers allow that expression is what makes them drinkable," he said. "I have lived twenty-two years in the Hudson Valley full time and I have a sense of place and a very special wine perspective. Rather than vineyards of grapes, we can look to have pear, apple and other fruit trees to cultivate. It is difficult to make great wine in the Hudson Valley with the weather, especially noble varietals given the winter, with the nice balance of sugar and acid we see from Europe where they make adjustments for complexity and elegance and finesse the production for the right balance and taste that produces value."

Recalling his first introduction to Hudson Valley wines, he said, "I remember in the mid '70 or '80s meeting Bill Wetmore from Cascade Mountain Winery, who was among the first with Clinton Vineyards to follow. Wetmore came into the game with lovely wines. Complex and dry, and with ambition if you will."

His insight is shared among the many great producers of regional wines. Terroir is everything, and the producer has to be patient and persevere despite the weather, research and variables in the Hudson Valley region. Rosenthal explained, "We have beautiful late summer and fall selections that are drinkable wines. Wonderfully dry with acidity. And as we look across the Hudson River—we see an experiment with black currants and Riesling that is very interesting. Price has to drive the balance from this kind of production."

Moving beyond the romance of vines, behind the scene in Cuomo's game-changing administration, local food and drink become *the* economic engine in our agricultural community. Bold changes make big headlines, as food and wine policies become common practice. And while our visionary governor leads, Samuel Filler is the most popular man in New York wine. He's behind the Taste NY signs on roadways and welcome centers and looks at how food and wine policy gets put into place. He's the go-to guy who doesn't disappoint.

Eleanor Roosevelt speaking at the dedication of the FDR home. *Photo by Abbie Rowe; courtesy of the National Archives and Records Administration.*

Officially, Sam Filler heads up Governor Cuomo's Craft Beverage Initiative at Empire State Development. At the Wine, Beer, Spirits and Cider Summit in October 2013, Governor Cuomo and his team announced a slew of changes, including a "one-stop shop" for New York craft beverage makers. Governor Cuomo conceived of this idea to provide New York's wine, beer and spirit producers with a single point of government contact for assistance regarding regulations, licensing, state incentives and any other questions or issues facing the industry. As a result of that 2013 summit, the one-stop shop also made available state financing options to the farm-based beverage industry and developed an online marketplace to connect farmers to beverage producers, a business mentor program for the craft beverage industry and state-operated webinars that are hosted on a variety of industry-related topics.

As a panelist at the American Farmland Trust discussion on Harvesting Opportunities for wines, beers, spirits and ciders in New York State, Filler provided answers and shared examples of what others were doing in the industry. He did the press and promotional rounds, appearing on WAMC radio and in other outlets to promote the industry. Filler's all-encompassing mission was to ensure that farm brewing, distilling, winemaking and cider-making industries are all part of a larger plan to aid New York agriculture through economic development, with an emphasis on the products that can be made from crops.

"As an orchard, instead of selling just raw apples, you can take them and turn them into a vodka, turn them into a brandy or turn them into a hard cider and get even more value out of them," Filler said.

Filler's vision and Governor Cuomo's new approach to local libations have produced a paradigm shift and opportunity for all, best explained by New York Wine and Grape Foundation president Jim Trezise. He explained, "I've often pinched myself in the past year or two to make sure I'm not dreaming when I'm dealing with the New York State government. I've been doing that for over thirty years, often with difficult and unpleasant encounters, but there has been a sea change under the leadership of Governor Andrew Cuomo."

The result of their dedication is more locals who are drinking local, job creation and a booming marketplace that helps us regain our agrarian roots and proudly wear the mantle of the first winemaking region in America.

Commissioner Richard Ball, Sam Filler, Pat Hooker, NYS Liquor Authority, Department of Ag & Markets and Governor Andrew Cuomo and his executive branch of advisors and administration—which also still includes John Dyson as a valued consultant of the current administration—are just a few of the key players, but there are dozens of assistants, publicists and canny marketers toiling behind the scenes to help turn the Hudson Valley wine region's reputation and future around.

New legislation is enabling New York's wine and agriculture industries to experience new heights. *Courtesy of Tessa Edick.*

Many of the incremental changes affect tiny fractions of the law but have surprisingly widely felt effects. "What you do on your own property has had so many restrictions in the past, but today you can have tasting rooms with an assortment of products encouraging growth of the industry. Where the odd quirks of how things had been, restrictions are getting cleaned up for collaborations and catapulting to make life easier to do business in New York State," Commissioner Ball explained.

Still other changes have liberalized cross-promotional efforts. Sam Filler said, "Governor Cuomo recognized the growing and captive industry rooted in the soil of our state. If you invest in a vineyard, it is a multi-year investment to New York State and creates jobs, so we want to invest in and support these businesses. There was a lot of onerous laws on books from alcohol beverage control laws—over six years modernized and liberalized these to explore promo and collaboration and better access to market more rights and privileges to using local ingredients. There are many many talented winemakers in Hudson Valley, and we are very fortunate to have Cornell University as our research institute."

Statewide promotion in the industry is working with wine trail organizations too. A wine and grape foundation trade association for wine industry has been around since 1985, when Governor Mario Cuomo started it. Since then, research for viticulture and oenology has been funded with Cornell University to reimagine the possibilities for varietals like Seyval Blanc and Cab Franc through crossbreeding and experimental plantings.

John Dyson was the New York commissioner of agriculture in 1975. A worldly man and founder of the Dyson School at Cornell University, he's a pioneer vintner in the Hudson Valley. "He laid the groundwork for others in the craft beverage industry, along with Dr. Konstantin Frank, another pioneer," Commissioner Richard Ball explained. "The world didn't believe grapes would grow here [in the Hudson Valley], but as we look back and today have over 420 wineries in New York State and won the designated wine region award of the year—we are now among the global producers and every year are better at our craft."

In 2017, Cab Franc will be going strong throughout the valley; we will see a rise in the number of New York State–produced wines at the table: Long Islands reds, outstanding new wineries in the capital region like Victory View (which overlooks the Saratoga Battle Grounds) and representation from the North Country with wineries like Fulkerson Winery in the Finger Lakes region. Each wine-growing region in New York has different strengths, and by celebrating all of them, the entire industry and state will be lifted up.

Head over to the charming, chic and always tasty tasting room at Tousey. *Courtesy of the Hudson-Berkshire Beverage Trail.*

The presence of New York–made wine in particular provides a change and opportunity to sample, touch, taste and get used to experiencing the connection to where your drinks come from.

Taste NY locations are often gateway points, airports, well-traveled highways, tourism destinations and welcome centers connecting visitors and locals to the people behind their locally grown food and drink. Stores located at Todd Hill along the Taconic Parkway, at Grand Central Station and in Long Island produced the numbers that prove New York is sourcing local products and spending on food that comes directly from our state dairies, livestock, grain, fiber, fruit and vegetable farms with an entrepreneurial spirit that is unparalleled. Many of these value-added products doubled, then tripled and doubled that tripled revenue again in only the third year since they began with a retail success that keeps consumers coming back to learn and taste more.

What started as Pride of NY celebrating farm-based wholesale production of bushels, totes and cases dovetailed into an evolving marketplace that is more interested than ever in local food and drink from the agriculturally rich Hudson Valley region. Finally, sustainably minded producers, strong advocates in Albany, a locally minded populace and hordes of curious visitors are coming together to make the program and the products that flow from it as irresistible and eagerly consumed as a well-earned glass of wine at the end of a hectic work week.

10

PERFECT PAIRINGS FROM HUDSON VALLEY CHEFS

HUDSON VALLEY FARM-TO-TABLE RESTAURANTS

*T*he question most hosts ask themselves once they settle on a menu for their dinner or party is what kind of wine should I serve? Selecting the perfect crisp dry Riesling to accompany the fresh cheese course, a spirited Cab Franc for the black pepper–crusted grass-fed flank steak and then a late-harvest Pinot Noir to complement the chocolate mousse seems almost as important as a delicious meal.

An entire cottage industry of books, courses and websites has sprung up around the art and science of choosing ideal food and wine combinations.

Pairing food and wine is a global pastime, and in the Hudson Valley, our chefs are more committed to the art than most. They are equally committed to producers of local libations as they are to family farms. With such an abundance of regional fruit to choose from for picking, pressing, fermenting and pairing with recipes, they are committed to the notion that what grows together goes together. Following are a few of our favorite restaurants in the region supporting local beyond the plate from local grain and fruit.

FISH & GAME, HUDSON, NEW YORK

Chef Zakary Pelaccio and Jori Jayne Emde

The 2016 James Beard Award for Best Chef Northeast went to Zakary Pelaccio of Fish & Game in Hudson, New York. The restaurant is perched

Savor the Hudson Valley landscape at sunset during FarmOn!'s Play with Fire event at Fish & Game Farm. *Courtesy of FarmOnFoundation.org.*

on the banks of the Hudson River and has become an urban oasis in the country with the Catskills Mountains as its backdrop for both its staff and its clients. (Zak, like many other creative people in the Hudson Valley, had a successful career in New York City before heading for the Hudson Valley for the physical, spiritual and mental space the countryside offers.) The town

Fish & Game is located in, Hudson, has evolved over the centuries from a commercial whaling town to a stomping ground for the Hudson River School of Painting and its current status as the capital of bohemian farm chic for Hollywood and Manhattan expats. Hudson has enjoyed an eclectic and varied history and has always remained connected to the land.

Fish & Game's wine list is focused on turning the philosophy of terroir into practice. *Wine Enthusiast* named Fish & Game one of America's best wine restaurants, calling the list "tightly focused" and praising the fact that it "highlights small producers who practice the same thoughtful farming practices that the restaurant demands of its food purveyors." Featuring regional hard ciders and nose-to-tail practices in the kitchen, the Fish & Game family features Hudson Valley libations and tastings on a regular basis, supported by the top producers in the region with a love for hard cider, which locally we consume like wine.

Terrapin Restaurant, Rhinebeck, New York

Wine Spectator's Award of Excellence winner and a driving force behind the Hudson Valley farm-to-table movement since 1998, Chef Josh Kroner

Cider, fruit wines and celebrations are the Hudson Valley winners. *Courtesy of FarmOnFoundation.org.*

celebrates robust local bounty at Terrapin, his Hudson Valley dining destination. Terrapin is located in a Baptist church (circa 1825) in Rhinebeck, New York, and the drama and beauty of the space are reflected on the menu.

Committed to recipes and wine pairings, Terrapin features flights of wine from local producers so diners can choose any four New York State wines to taste and pair with their food. Millbrook Winery's Tocai Friulano is even on tap. It's a favorite among locals that Chef Kroner insists "keeps getting better," often urging diners who are unfamiliar with the region's wines to at least try it.

"There are some really good wines in the Hudson Valley," Chef Kroner explained. "What Whitehall does is incredible, the product is unbelievable and Millbrook and

Tousey Wineries—they are making really great wines! Clinton Vineyard offers good selections from years of winemaking. They were pioneers."

Maple Brined Grilled Pork Chops
with Calvados Demi-Glace and Maple-Bacon Almonds

By Chef Josh Kroner

Chef Josh Kroner shared the following recipe and recommended Millbrook Winery's Tocai Friulano, Tousey's rosé or Benmarl's Cab Franc to serve with the dish.

For new and experienced Hudson Valley wine drinkers, Kroner's top picks are "Tousey rosé, Benmarl Cab Franc, both listed on my wine list and both able to withstand terroir and torture of temperature here."

Like many other tastemakers in the Hudson Valley, Chef Kroner is particularly enthusiastic about the magical things happening with the Cab Franc grape and the region's terroir of late. "Years ago, Millbrook was the only acceptable Cab Franc I'd put on my menu, but today, there are great local selections like Fulkerson Winery from the Finger Lakes and Yankee Folly Cidery in New Paltz," he said.

These pork chops take full advantage of the rich flavor of Crown Maple's dark amber maple syrup. First, the chops are soaked in a brine made from Crown Maple and sea salt. Next, the rich calvados demi-glace is finished with Crown Maple to accentuate the apple and spice notes. Finally, the dish is finished with chopped maple-bacon nuts that provide a little crunch and Crown Maple's dark amber syrup, which highlights the toasted almond flavor.

The Brine

½ gallon water, room temperature
½ cup sea salt
2 cups Crown Maple dark amber syrup
½ gallon ice water
6 (16- to 20-ounce) pork chops

Mix room-temperature water with salt and maple syrup. Add ice water and pork chops. Place in a container that will fit in your refrigerator. Keep refrigerated for 24 hours.

Calvados Apple Demi-Glace

5 local Hudson Valley apples
2 quarts chicken stock
½ cup Calvados
3 cinnamon sticks
5 cloves
1 tablespoon butter
1 tablespoon Crown Maple dark amber syrup
Salt and pepper, to taste

Cut the apples in half and place in a large heavy-bottom saucepan along with the stock, Calvados, cinnamon and cloves. Bring to a boil on high heat and continue to boil until the stock is reduced to approximately 1 cup. This might take an hour, depending on the amount of heat the pan is on. When the sauce appears to be close, reduce heat to low, so not to over reduce. Add the butter by swirling in with a spoon and then add the maple syrup and season to taste with salt and pepper. Reserve sauce.

Maple-Bacon Almonds

1 egg
1 cup whole almonds
2 tablespoons Crown Maple dark amber syrup
2 teaspoons kosher salt
1 slice thick-cut bacon, cooked and finely chopped

Preheat oven to 350 degrees. Separate the egg, placing the white in a stainless-steel bowl and reserving the yolk for another use. Whip the egg white with a whisk until it forms soft peaks. Add almonds, maple syrup, salt and chopped bacon and mix well. Spread evenly over a baking pan. Cook for 12 minutes, mixing almonds to promote even cooking after 6 minutes. Remove from oven and cool, then coarsely chop and reserve.

Remove pork chops from brine and dry with towel. Sprinkle with freshly ground pepper and cook on a hot grill until both sides are evenly marked. Place chops in a 350-degree oven and cook to an internal temperature of 150 degrees. To serve, place one chop on a plate and pour 4 tablespoons of sauce over and sprinkle with the chopped almonds. Serves 6.

Bartlett House, Kitchen, Bakery & Café, Ghent, New York

Obsessed with the quality of each element that goes into the making and shaping of everything they do, Bartlett House takes inspiration from our community, welcoming guests with approachable and seasonal plates that aim to create a holistic Hudson Valley cuisine. Through the application of diverse flavors and tastes, they celebrate the building's history as a crossroads of people and culture. With a collaborative spirit, Bartlett House is nourished by relationships with local farmers, producers and growers. In a constant state of creation, the entire team meets weekly to develop and explore new recipes, daily specials and innovations around the table and in the kitchen.

Short Ribs at Bartlett House with Sunchoke Potato Puree
Wine Pairing: Hudson Valley Cab Franc

5 (2.5-inch) beef short ribs
Salt
Pepper
⅛ cup vegetable or canola oil
4 shallots, coarsely chopped
1 carrot, coarsely chopped
½ head celery, coarsely chopped
4 cloves garlic, smashed
2 sprigs thyme
¼ can tomato paste
1 cup dry red wine
2 quarts beef stock

Trim the short ribs and season with salt and pepper on each side. Warm oil over medium high heat in a rondeau or Dutch oven. Add the short ribs and sear on each side until evenly browned and reserve.

Add the vegetables and thyme and sauté in the same pan the short ribs were cooked in. Add the tomato paste and toss to coat. Add the red wine to the vegetables and tomato paste. Reduce by half and add the beef stock.

Immerse short ribs in the beef stock and vegetables, cover with aluminum foil and place in a 275-degree oven for 3 to 4 hours until a fork or knife can be inserted into the short rib. Strain out the vegetables and place the stock in a sauce pan and reduce by half.

Sunchoke and Potato Puree

4 medium-sized potatoes
2 to 4 sunchokes
Water
1 tablespoon salt
1 cup heavy cream
4 tablespoons butter
Parsley, chopped

Peel potatoes and sunchokes. Fill a saucepan with water and add a tablespoon of salt. Add potatoes and sunchokes and bring to a boil. Cook until tender. Remove from heat and drain. Warm cream and butter and pour over potatoes and sunchokes. Mash together to combine.

Ladle puree into a bowl, place 2 short ribs on top and drizzle with sauce. Garnish with chopped parsley.
Yield: 4 to 8 people

Market Street, Rhinebeck, New York

Another Hudson Valley food and wine hot spot is Market Street, nestled in the heart of the Hudson Valley in historic Rhinebeck. Opened in 2012, it is the second restaurant from the team of Chef Gianni Scappin and Lois Freedman to offer Chef Scappin's lauded contemporary Italian menu, featuring seasonal, local ingredients combined with the highest-quality Italian products.

The wine specials on the chalkboard celebrate local juice. Chardonnay and Pinot Noir are both on tap, and the nationally awarded Tocai Friulano is by the bottle. All are from Millbrook Winery and recommended for pairing here with the famed bruschetta so beloved at Market Street.

Peposo Bruschetta with Butternut Squash
By Chef Giovanni Scappin
Wine Pairing: Tocai Friulano

2 medium onions, diced
2 celery stalks, sliced
1 garlic bulb, smashed (about 6 cloves)
½ cup extra virgin olive oil
1 (3-pound) bone-out beef shank, cubed
1 (3-ounce) can tomato paste
1 (750-milliliter) bottle red wine (Millbrook recommended)
2 bay leaves
8 sage leaves, chopped
1 sprig rosemary leaves, chopped
1¼ tablespoons coarsely ground black pepper
1½ tablespoons kosher salt
1 (1-pound) medium butternut squash, peeled and cleaned
Butter or olive oil for tossing the squash
Bread (crusty)
Balsamic vinegar tradizionale to taste
Pepper to taste
Celery leaves for garnish

Heat oven to 300 to 325 degrees. In a small casserole, sweat onion, celery and garlic cloves in oil for about 10 to 12 minutes until well cooked and lightly colored. Add beef and stir for about 5 minutes well. Add tomato paste, and after 2 to 3 minutes, add the wine, herbs, pepper and salt. Cover with a lid and place in oven for about 2½ hours or until done and very soft. Remove meat and, if necessary, reduce sauce. Remove bay leaves.

Toss butternut squash with butter or oil and roast on a small sheet pan for about 15 minutes at 375 to 400 degrees Fahrenheit until lightly caramelized. Set aside.

Fall harvest in the Hudson Valley is for large vineyards and small homesteads. *Courtesy of FarmOnFoundation.org.*

To order, grill bread well and top with the broken pieces of stewed beef. Spoon over a bit of the sauce and top with the roasted butternut squash, lightly drizzle with few drops of aged balsamic vinegar tradizionale. Garnish with more freshly ground coarse black pepper and a few leaves of celery.

Yield: 6–8 servings depending on size and course

THE VILLAGE TEA ROOM RESTAURANT AND BAKESHOP, NEW PALTZ, NEW YORK

Chef Agnes Devereux is also passionate about pairing the perfect local wine with her from-scratch delicious French-style bistro fare. Aficionados of traditional French baked goods head to Chef Devereux of the Village Tea Room Restaurant and Bakeshop in New Paltz, who is more than happy to provide recommendations on the perfect local tipple to accompany her seasonal menu.

Chef Devereux recommends pairing Awosting White from Whitecliff Vineyard in Gardiner, New York, with her delicious tart, dense with potatoes cooked in cream and herbs and redolent of Toussaint cheese.

The Frontenac is a hybrid pioneered in a crossbreeding program at the University of Minnesota. It is a vigorous producer and resists pests. *Courtesy of the Hudson-Berkshire Beverage Trail.*

Chef explained this recipe was "inspired by an après ski tart from the Savoyard region of France. Perfect for an après climb in the Gunks! Toussaint Cheese is a raw milk cheese from Sprout Creek Farm in Poughkeepsie. Ronnybrook Farm and Evans Farmhouse Creamery sell the excellent dairy, a thick yellow cream and milk that gives this tart a rich old-world flavor."

Chef pairs it with her kale salad, which features Jacuterie maple- and sea salt–cured bacon, local kale, roasted sweet red onions and shaved Clothbound Cheddar from Hawthorne Valley Farm in Ghent. (You can find that recipe on her blog, wordofmouthhv.com.)

Toussaint and Potato Tart with Pate Brisée
By Chef Agnes Devereux
Wine Pairing: Awosting White from Whitecliff Vineyard

Pate Brisée

½ pound butter
12 ounces unbleached un-bromated all-purpose flour
½ teaspoon kosher salt
¼ teaspoon baking powder
3 ounces cold filtered water

Cut the butter into 6–8 pieces. Combine the dry ingredients and the butter in the bowl of a mixer with the paddle attachment on lowest speed, leaving pieces of butter no more than ¼ of an inch across. Stir in water until dough *just* holds together. Scrape out of bowl. Shape into two flat discs. Wrap in plastic. Chill until firm.

Filling

2 pounds Yukon Gold potatoes chopped thin in medallions
10 ounces whole milk (non-homogenized, no ultra pasteurized)
8 ounces heavy cream (no ultra pasteurized)
2 sprigs thyme
2 cloves garlic, peeled and lightly crushed
Salt
Pepper
½ ounce butter

1 medium onion, diced into ½-inch pieces
1 organic egg
¼ teaspoon nutmeg
8 ounces Sprout Creek Farm Toussaint cheese, crust removed and cut into ⅛-inch-thick slices

Line springform pan with pate brisée and freeze for one hour. Preheat oven to 350 degrees. Bake blind until lightly browned, 20 minutes weighted with beans or ceramic pie weights and 10 minutes without. Combine potatoes with 8 ounces milk, cream, 1 sprig of thyme and a garlic clove. Season with salt and pepper and bring to a boil. Lower heat and simmer for 25 to 30 minutes or until potatoes are tender. Discard thyme and garlic and let potatoes cool in the liquid.

Warm the butter in a pan over medium to low heat and add the onion, remaining thyme and garlic and more salt and pepper. Cook until the onions are translucent and tender, about 18 to 20 minutes. Add a little water if pan gets too dry.

Remove from heat, discard thyme and garlic and set aside to cool.

Drain the potatoes, straining the milk and cream into a liquid measuring cup. Add enough extra milk to equal 10 ounces if necessary.

In a bowl, whisk together egg and nutmeg and then add to the milk and cream mixture. Season with salt and pepper and whisk to combine.

Scatter half the onions, half the potatoes and half the Toussaint in blind-baked tart shell. Then add remaining onions and potatoes. Top with the rest of the cheese. Pour the milk and cream mixture over the filling and cover pan with foil. Make sure foil is tented and not touching the surface of the tart.

Bake for about 45 minutes, remove foil and bake an additional 15 minutes. Let cool for 2 hours before serving.

The Roundhouse, Beacon, New York

Sleep tight. *Courtesy of the Hudson-Berkshire Beverage Trail.*

Chef Terrance Brennan started cooking as a teenager, working in his father's small restaurant in the suburbs of Washington, D.C. From there, he made his way to famed New York City restaurant Le Cirque and then to Europe for two years of cooking at the most prestigious Michelin-starred restaurants. After returning to the United States, Chef Brennan opened Picholine, which earned him three stars from the *New York Times*, four stars from *New York Magazine* and two stars in the Michelin Guide. He went on to open Artisanal and the Artisanal Premium Cheese Center, a facility dedicated to the world's finest cheeses. Chef Brennan's move to the Hudson Valley has greatly influenced his approach to cooking and inspired the creation of his new restaurant at the Roundhouse. The historic Roundhouse by Chef Brennan is located in Beacon, New York, on a waterfall, and it embodies the reason we eat out in the Hudson Valley. Locally inspired American fare with a spectacular setting (set in a chic boutique hotel, lounge, bar and spectacular event space), the Roundhouse offers a whole farm-inspired menu that features cuisine celebrating the agricultural richness of the region. Passionately committed to sustainability and supporting local farms, wineries, distillers and producers, each of Chef Brennan's unique dishes and libations is crafted with care beyond the plate.

Whole Roasted Cauliflower with Harissa Sauce
by Chef Terrance Brennan
Wine Pairing: Anything from the amazing beverage craftsmen of the Hudson Valley wineries, distilleries and cideries

Harissa Sauce

¾ cup harissa paste (Mina brand)
3 teaspoons salt
3 teaspoons honey

2 teaspoons lemon juice
¼ cup extra virgin olive oil

Combine harissa with salt, honey and lemon juice. Slowly whisk in olive oil.

Roasted Cauliflower

2 tablespoons extra virgin olive oil
1 whole white cauliflower, trimmed and leaves removed
Harissa sauce
1 cup water
3 tablespoons butter
4 tablespoons coarse chiffonade mint leaves
3 tablespoons coarse chiffonade parsley
3 tablespoons sliced almonds
3 tablespoons golden raisins

Preheat oven to 350 degrees. In a 10-inch sauté pan, brush olive oil to coat the bottom, place cauliflower in center and pour ½ cup harissa sauce on top of the cauliflower. Using a pastry brush, spread the sauce all over, making sure the entire cauliflower is covered.

Add 1 cup of water to the bottom of the pan, place in the oven on the middle rack and cook for approximately 1 hour and 15 minutes, basting every 20 minutes with the sauce on the bottom of the pan. The cauliflower is done when a skewer can penetrate through without any resistance.

Place a 10-inch sauté pan over medium to high heat and allow the pan to get hot. Add butter; when it begins to turn brown and foam, add the mint and parsley and swirl the butter and herbs in the pan for about 30 seconds or until the herbs become crispy.

Add the almonds and cook for another 30 seconds, add the raisins and remove from heat.

Whisk in remaining harissa. Place the cauliflower on a plate, pour over the harissa sauce and serve.

Crew Restaurant, Poughkeepsie, New York

Delivering one of Hudson Valley's most genuine farm-to-table experiences from local farms and backyard garden, Chef Tom Kacherski (a CIA graduate) and his wife, Becky, share a passion for local, organic ingredients and dedication to dining excellence in this gem of a restaurant. Crew is so dedicated to local cooking that the team capitalizes on a patch of land out back and source as much seasonal, fresh produce as they can from the garden planted there. Shrimp and linguini Corsara is a tomato pesto sauce with a touch of wine and cream. It would pair very nicely with wines from Millbrook. The Hunt Country Rose and the Pinot Noir are Chef Tom's favorites.

Shrimp and Linguini Corsara
By Chef Tom Kacherski
Wine Pairing: Chardonnay by Millbrook Winery

1 ½ ounces extra virgin olive oil
4 to 8 shrimp, tail on or off, your choice
2 to 3 cloves of garlic, sliced thinly
2 ounces white wine
5 ounces marinara/tomato sauce
2 tablespoons pesto
1 ounce heavy cream
Kosher/sea salt, to taste
Fresh ground black pepper, to taste
Prepared pasta

Heat a 10-inch sauté pan on medium-high heat, add olive oil. Meanwhile, season shrimp with salt and pepper. Once the oil is hot, add shrimp and cook on both sides until 80 percent cooked. Remove the shrimp from pan and reserve. Add garlic and cook briefly, with very little color on garlic. Deglaze the pan with the white wine, add tomato sauce and simmer for a couple minutes. Add the pesto and cream; season to taste. Pour over linguini or your favorite pasta. You can also substitute chicken breast cut up for the shrimp.

Café of Love, Mount Kisco, New York

Café of Love in Mount Kisco, New York, is bringing Hudson Valley farm-to-table ingredients on a global adventure. Leslie Lampert's spin-off of her award-winning soup shop, Ladle of Love, has received accolades from *Zagat*, *Westchester Magazine*, the *Journal News* and the *New York Times*, which called the Café "an engaging little restaurant…with an appealing blend of rusticity and sophistication, contemporary without being modern." The kitchen team turns up the heat nightly, featuring the freshest farm fare in all its seasonal glory complete with regional wine pairings. If you are interested in a casual supper or a gastronomic feast, stop in and leave your passports at home.

Jurassic Pork Shanks
By Chef Leslie Lampert
Wine Pairing: Heron Hill or Millbrook Vineyard

6 (1½-pound) pork shanks
Kosher salt
Freshly ground pepper
¼ cup olive oil
1 medium onion, chopped
2 medium carrots, chopped
2 parsnips, chopped
2 medium celery ribs, chopped
½ head red cabbage, shredded
6 garlic cloves, minced
2 heaping tablespoons tomato paste
1 cup dry red wine
6 cups chicken stock or beef stock
3 rosemary sprigs
6 thyme sprigs
3 bay leaves
¼ cup cornstarch
Water

Season shanks liberally with salt and pepper. In a large skillet, heat 2 tablespoons of the olive oil until shimmering. Add 3 of the pork shanks and cook over moderately high heat until browned all over, about 10 minutes. Transfer the browned shanks to a deep, heavy casserole dish. Wipe out the skillet and brown the remaining 3 pork shanks in the remaining 2 tablespoons of olive oil. Add the pork shanks to the casserole. Add the onion, carrots, parsnips, celery, cabbage and garlic to the skillet and cook over moderate heat until softened, about 5 minutes. Add the tomato paste and toast for a couple of minutes, stirring. Add the wine and bring to a boil. Simmer until slightly reduced, about 2 minutes. Pour the wine and vegetables over the pork. Add the stock, rosemary, thyme and bay leaves, seasoning again with salt and pepper, and bring to a boil. Tuck the pork shanks into the liquid so they are submerged. Cover and cook over medium low heat for 2½ hours or until the meat is very tender. Turn the pork shanks every 30 minutes to keep them submerged in the liquid. Mix the cornstarch with equal amount water to make a slurry. Whisk slurry into liquid and simmer until thickened. Transfer the braised shanks to a large, deep platter, skim any fat off gravy and surround shanks with vegetables. Garnish with thyme and rosemary sprigs. Serve with local Hudson Valley wine.

The most lauded and beloved Hudson Valley chefs are rallying behind their local winemakers, because they've discovered that serving wines grown and made in the same region their food is made is one of the oldest and surest ways to ensure menu harmony and integrated community. (It bears repeating: what grows together, goes together.) It's time to carry the movement to New York City. Manhattan and Brooklyn chefs are already utilizing Hudson Valley farm produce, dairy and meat. But they're dragging their feet on Hudson Valley wine as locally produced beer and spirits are celebrated at the bar.

Think of how much of a PR, feel-good and financial boost food and wine buyers at popular, well-regarded restaurants in New York City are regularly making on farmers' bottom lines. Think of how rapturously their dedications to local farmers on menus are read and absorbed. One big restaurant's financial commitment could literally raise up and support an entire winery, all of the people it employs and, by extension, the community they reside in.

The critical praise, the simplifying of licensing requirements and the ceaseless promotion of the wine industry in the Hudson Valley have undeniably enriched the present state of wine in the Hudson Valley. But there's something somewhat ineffable and difficult to articulate that also seems to be a big factor—and will ensure the future.

In the past ten years, thanks to a changing economy, shifting priorities in life and work, a new understanding of sustainability and a drive to educate ourselves and our children about the benefits of supporting local industry in all its forms, we are reexamining what's in our pantries, closets and, yes, liquor cabinets.

Should we be buying food grown in America but flown to China to be processed and packaged and then sent back to our grocery shelves? Should we be wearing clothes manufactured under questionable conditions in factories across the world? Should we be guzzling whiskey from Ireland, wine from France and beer from Germany?

The answer, of course, is no, at least not all the time. The extreme alternative—living in a locally made yurt, raising goats and learning how to make cheese, clothing from fiber we loomed ourselves and drinking some sort of fermented apple juice hooch experiment—is equally unappetizing.

More and more of us are seeking a middle road in an age of extremes, supporting our local everything, when we can, as often as we can. Producers of all stripes are meeting us halfway. Winemakers are finding ways to grow better grapes that are suitable not only to the climate but also to our palates and our wallets.

And legislators in New York are, if anything, leading the way for all of us. A bill that crossed Governor Cuomo's desk in late 2016 and is not getting much attention (but should) is one that allows for the creation and operation of custom wineries, cideries and breweries. While that may not sound like a revolution in a bottle, this legislation could have as much long-term effect on the success of farm-to-bottle wineries as the much-lauded Farm Winery Act of 1976.

Thanks to the new law, it is now legal in New York State to operate a shared production facility that home winemakers and brewers can tap into. Senator David Carlucci of Rockland County, who sponsored the bill, designed it so that it would benefit many sectors. Established wine and beer makers are now allowed to rent out their space and equipment to folks (frequently farmers) interested in creating lines of their own but without the space or capital to launch their own business quite yet. The program creates incubators giving would-be brewers and winemakers access to professional equipment and industry mavens, and it benefits the established players by bringing in a new stream of income.

The memo to the Senate bill breaks it down:

> [The legislation creates] *a new custom beermakers' center license that authorizes the operation of a custom beermakers' center facility to provide*

Women with the Hudson Standard Shrub. *Courtesy of FarmOnFoundation.org.*

> *individuals with rental space (to make and store homemade beer), the use*
> *of equipment and storage facilities, and/or beer making supplies for the*
> *production of beer for personal household use and not for commercial use*
> *or resale purposes. It defines beer making supplies as products grown or*
> *produced in New York in quantity amounts as determined by the State*
> *Liquor Authority. A custom beermakers' center licensee would be authorized,*
> *if permitted by the Federal Alcohol and Tobacco Tax and Trade Bureau*
> *(TTB), to conduct training classes on how to manufacture beer and conduct*
> *certain tastings of beer produced on the premises.*

The bill's effect on the cider and wine industry is identical.

We've seen what can happen in the food movement when lawmakers and locavores collaborate. The Know Your Farmer, Know Your Food movement has helped foster food hubs, farmers' markets and transparent field-to-store sourcing chains. School gardens are sprouting. Communities, students and farmers are benefiting. Now, we're starting to see the same enthusiasm spill over into the beverage world.

As the birthplace of American wine, as the region that has arguably seen the biggest uptick in critical approval thanks to its unique blend of natural terroir and scientific innovation, a region of unparalleled physical beauty and cultural resources, the Hudson Valley is uniquely poised to (sustainably!) capitalize on this enthusiasm and forward momentum.

Maybe Baco Noir is your jam, or maybe you want to grab a *Wine Enthusiast*–approved Cab Franc. More of a DIYer? You're in good company in the

We love ice wine from our local homestead winemakers of Trevor Valley Farm Winery. *Courtesy of Mike Rietbrock and Susan Pearson.*

Hudson Valley. Make your own wine—we offer resources and coursework with partners through Empire Farm; contact us at 518.329.FARM.

It truly is up to the consumer: the sustainability of farmers, winemakers and even the viability of healthy communities themselves that live and die for the responsible buying choices we make on a daily basis. Don't underestimate the very real power your drinking dollars make. And drink responsibly! Salute New York! FarmOn!

ACKNOWLEDGEMENTS

100 percent of the royalties from this book will go to support FarmOnFoundation.org. Visit us at Empire Farm in Copake, New York. Farm, eat and drink local!

Thank you, from Tessa Edick: Gratitude beyond words to the FarmOn! Foundation Board of Directors and Advisors who reminds me that success is the reward for daring to dream about changing the way we eat with food education and farm preservation to inspire the next generation to feed us! With tremendous gratitude and inspiration for my wine-loving friends, farmers and chosen FarmOn! family, I wouldn't be where I am today without you. To my lover, my brother, my mentors and farm sisters, please know you are in my heart, and this is cheers to you!! Kathleen Willcox, this is for you, your tireless smile and fun attitude—it's amazing, thank you for all you do! Tara Boyles, I thank the universe for you every day for your awesome spirit and getirdone way; you slay. Stephen, Jenna, John and Christy Mack, thank you doesn't begin to express the heartfelt gratitude, inspiration, joy and generosity you bring me every day. Joyce, John and Thea Varvatos, thank you for love, creativity, commitment, support and kindness. Marc Szafran, our hearts beat forever in joy with a sniff of terroir and a taste of possibility. Kipp Edick, for many a late night pondering the purpose and possibilities of growing up and making something out of nothing, thank you and saluté. EW in my heart with love always. Chazz and Howard with tremendous gratitude and guidance, thank you! Chris and Nanci Ross Weaver, to think a penny can lead to the most amazing connection with much love, direction and many thanks. Lois Krasilovsky and Scott Annan, you make the world a better place and bring joy to life—thank you for your time and support. Ross Mauri, thanks for showing me the way to Millbrook Winery and teaching me life is better with a beautiful red! Stacey Hengsterman and Chancellor Nancy Zimpher, thank you for believing in me and (local) wine at lunch you gorgeous, unstoppable duo! For the love of all things local and my many European wine travels, a heartfelt thank-you to Peter Jones and Sergio Poeta. And the Tiara Club. I would also like to thank Arcadia Publishing and The History Press, photo contributors, Trevor Valley Farm, New York State governor Andrew Cuomo, Jim Malatras, Sam Filler, Commissioner Richard Ball, Neal Rosenthal and Hudson Valley chefs, makers, growers and producers for lending their talent, work ethic and deliciously local recipes and wine pairings.

Thank you, from Kathleen Willcox: I would like to thank, first and foremost, my parents, Emily and Christopher, who taught me the art of understanding, discerning and relishing the fullness of life's major and minor joys, all of which were served up with heaving goblets of wine and splitting sides of laughter. I would also like to thank my partner in life and love, Stephen Repsher, who has been a constant source of support through the highs and lows of our journey together. My children, Emily and Miles, exemplify the reasons we need to continue pushing forward in the preservation of our state's great cultural heritage; you are my heart and my greatest hope for the future. Linda Pierro, Lydia Higginson and Karen Gardy, you were invaluable in providing your wise counsel. Our editor Amanda Irle politely steered us away from disaster on several occasions—thank you! To Daniella Deutsch, our intern, we could not have done it without you. Tessa, I will never forget the steady and unwavering commitment you devoted to this project. You are an inspiration!

HUDSON VALLEY WINERIES

Adair Vineyards
52 Alhusen Road, New Paltz, NY 12561
(845) 255-1377
adairwine.com

Altamont Winery
3001 Furbeck Road, Altamont, NY 12009
(518) 355-8100
altamontwinery.com

Amorici Vineyard and Winery Valley Falls
637 Colonel Burch Road, Valley Falls, NY 12185
(518) 469-0680
amoricivineyard.com

Annadale Cidery
8 David Way, Red Hook, NY 12571
cideralliance.com/members/annandale-cidery

Applewood Winery
82 Four Corners Road, Warwick, NY 10990
(845) 988-9292
applewoodwinery.com

Baldwin Vineyards
176 Hardenburgh Road, Pine Bush, NY 12566
(845) 744-2226
baldwinvineyards.com

Bashakill Vineyards
1131 S Road, Wurtsboro, NY 12790
(845) 888-5858
bashakillvineyards.com

Benmarl Winery
156 Highland Avenue, Marlboro, NY 12542
(845) 236-4265
benmarl.com

Brimstone Hill Vineyards
61 Brimstone Hill Road, Pine Bush, NY 12566
(845) 744-2231
brimstonehillwinery.com

Brookview Station Winery
1297 Brookview Station Road, Castleton, NY 12033
(518) 732-7495
brookviewstationwinery.com

Brotherhood, America's Oldest Winery
100 Brotherhood Plaza Drive, Washingtonville, NY 10992
(845) 496-3661
brotherhood-winery.com

Cascade Mountain Winery
835 Cascade Mountain Road, Amenia, NY 12501
(845) 373-9021
cascademt.com

Catskill Distilling Company
2037 NY-17B, Bethel, NY 12720
(845) 583-3141
catskilldistilling.com

Cereghino Smith
PO Box 193 2583 Route 32, Bloomington, NY 12411-0193
(845) 334-8282
cereghinosmith.com

Clearview Vineyard
35 Clearview Lane, Warwick, NY 10990
(845) 651-2838
clearviewvineyard.com

Clinton Vineyards
450 Schultzville Road, Clinton Corners, NY 12514
(845) 266-5372
clintonvineyards.com

Colebrook Country Wines
Colebrook Road, Gansevoort, NY 12831
(518) 261-1877
catchwine.com/wineries/new_york/colebrook_country_wines

Demarest Hill Winery
81 Pine Island Turnpike, Warwick, NY 10990
(845) 986-4723
demaresthillwinery.com

El Paso Winery
742 Broadway, Ulster Park, NY 12487
(845) 331-8642
elpasowinery.com

Enlightenment Wines
93 Scott Avenue, Brooklyn, NY 11237
(401) 481-9205
enlightenmentwines.com

Glorie Farm Winery
40 Mountain Road, Marlboro, NY 12542
(845) 236-3265
gloriewine.com

Harvest Spirits Inc.
3074 U.S. 9, Valatie, NY 12184
(518) 758-1776
harvestspirits.com

Hudson-Chatham Winery
1900 NY-66, Ghent, NY 12075
(518) 392-9463
hudsonchathamwinery.com

Johnston's Winery Inc.
5140 Bliss Road, Ballston Spa, NY 12020
(518) 882-6310
upperhudsonvalleywinetrail.com/wineries/johnstons-winery2

Ledge Rock Hill Winery
41 Stewart Dam Road, Corinth, NY 12822
(518) 654-5467
lrhwinery.com

Magnanini Farm Winery
172 Strawridge Road, Wallkill, NY 12589
(845) 895-2767
magwine.com

Millbrook Vineyard and Winery
26 Wing Road, Millbrook, NY 12545
(845) 677-8383
millbrookwine.com

Mountain View Winery
14831 Pierce Road, Saratoga, NY 95070
(408) 741-2822
mountainwinery.com

Nostrano Vineyards
14 Gala Lane, Milton, NY 12547
(845) 795-5473
nostranovineyards.com

Oak Summit Vineyard
372 Oak Summit Road, Millbrook, NY 12545
(845) 677-9522

Oliva Vineyards
240 Excelsior Avenue, Saratoga Springs, NY 12866
(518) 350-4515
olivavineyards.com

Palaia Vineyards
10 Sweet Clover Road, Highland Mills, NY 10930
(845) 928-5384
palaiavineyards.com

Pazdar Winery
Scotchtown, NY
pazdarwinery.com

Prospero Winery
134 Marble Avenue, Pleasantville, NY 10570
(914) 769-6870
prosperowinery.com

Robibero Family Vineyard
714 Albany Post Road, New Paltz, NY 12561
(845) 255-9463
robiberofamilyvineyards.com

Royal Kedem Winery
1519 Route 9W, Marlboro, NY 12542
(845) 236-3651
kedemwinery.com

The Saratoga Winery
462 NY-29, Saratoga Springs, NY 12866
(518) 584-9463
thesaratogawinery.com

Slyboro Cider House Granville
18 Hicks Road, Granville, NY 12832
(518) 642-1788
slyboro.com

Stoutridge Vineyards
10 Ann Kaley Lane, Marlboro, NY 12542
(845) 236-7620
stoutridge.com

Suarez Family Brewery
Livingston, NY
suarezfamilybrewery.com

Tousey Winery
1774 U.S. 9 #1, Germantown, NY 12526
(518) 567-5462
touseywinery.com

Trevor Valley Farm
Ancram, NY
trevorvalleyfarm.com

Tuthilltown Spirits
14 Grist Mill Lane, Gardiner, NY 12525
(845) 255-1527
tuthilltown.com

Victory View Vineyard
11975 NY-40, Schaghticoke, NY 12154
(518) 461-7132
victoryviewvineyard.com

Warwick Valley Winery Distillery
114 Little York Road, Warwick, NY 10990
(845) 258-4858
wvwinery.com

Whitecliff Vineyard and Winery
331 Mckinstry Road, Gardiner, NY 12525
(845) 255-4613
whitecliffwine.com

HUDSON VALLEY WINE TRAILS

1. DUTCHESS WINE TRAIL

The Dutchess Wine Trail is located in eastern Dutchess County and connects Clinton Vineyards and Millbrook Vineyards and Winery. The two wineries are within fifteen minutes' driving time of each other. On the trail, visitors will find vineyards, orchards and farms that provide the bounty of this beautiful valley. Other local treasures include Innisfree Garden, the Culinary Institute of America and the FDR Library and Home.

Wineries

Clinton Vineyards
Millbrook Vineyards and Winery

For more information: dutchesswinetrail.com

2. HUDSON–BERKSHIRE BEVERAGE TRAIL

The Hudson-Berkshire Beverage Trail is located right in between the Hudson Valley and the Berkshire Mountains, leading all the way from the southeastern part of Albany to Hudson, New York. The trail carries handcrafted wines, beers, spirits and even renowned wines that have won awards. Additionally, the trail provides fresh and local produce, artisanal cheeses, baked goods, 100 percent natural maple syrup, fresh apple ciders and even more local food

Wineries

Berkshire Mountain Distillers
Brookview Station Winery
Clermont Vineyards & Winery
Furnace Brook Winery
Harvest Spirits
Hillrock Distillery
Hudson-Chatham Winery
Hudson Valley Distillers

For more information: hudsonberkshireexperience.com

3. SHAWANGUNK WINE TRAIL

The Shawangunk Wine Trail includes fifteen wineries between the Shawangunk Mountains and the Hudson River, located a short sixty miles north of New York City.

The family-owned wineries are on the small to medium side, located from New Paltz in Ulster County to Warwick in Orange County. The wineries produce award-winning white wine, red wine and distilled spirits.

Wineries

Adair Vineyards
Applewood Winery
Baldwin Vineyards
Benmarl Winery
Brimstone Hill Vineyard
Brotherhood Winery
Brunel & Rafael Winery
Clearview Vineyard

Demarest Hill Winery and Distillery
Glorie Farm Winery
Palaia Vineyards and Winery
Robibero Winery
Stoutridge Vineyards
Warwick Valley Winery and Distillery
Whitecliff Vineyard

For more information: shawangunkwinetrail.com

4. UPPER HUDSON WINE TRAIL

The Upper Hudson Wine Trail spans from Grandma Moses country in Washington County to the horse racing country in Saratoga County all the way to the Queen of American Lakes in Warren County. The wineries are located a short distance from New York City, Boston and Montreal. In addition, they are only a short drive from Albany and Glens Falls, New York, and western Vermont.

Wineries

Adirondack Winery
Amorici Vineyard
The Fossil Stone Vineyards
Galway Rock Vineyard and Winery
Johnston's Winery
Ledge Rock Hill Winery and Vineyard
Oliva Vineyards
The Saratoga Winery
Swedish Hill Winery
Thirsty Owl Saratoga
Victory View Vineyard

For more information: hudsonriverwine.blogspot.com/2013/01/saratogian-upper-hudson-valley-wine.html

WINE TRAIL EVENTS

*E*very winery features annual events that are well worth a visit. Check out their websites (see Appendix A) and sign up for newsletters for special discounts on tickets. The following are just a few of our favorite annual events, but there are many more.

DUTCHESS WINE TRAIL
Events

GRAND PORTFOLIO TASTING

The entire Millbrook wine portfolio (as well as a few wines from Villa Pillo and Williams Selyem) is opened for a very special annual wine tasting that kicks off each holiday season. This wine tasting event is a unique experience for wine lovers and Millbrook fans and typically held in early December.

HUDSON–BERKSHIRE BEVERAGE TRAIL
Events

BATTLE FOR THE BEST LOCAL CRAFT COCKTAIL

Typically held in the middle of May in Quincy, Massachusetts, the Battle usually features many Hudson Valley producers.

FARMON! AT EMPIRE FARM HOOT! (Typically held at the end of July in Copake, New York)
A farm fresh Hootenanny! benefit dinner featuring food and wine produced within five miles of your plate and local libations of all kinds from celebrity chefs celebrating family farms and funding youth education in agriculture for 501c3 FarmOnFoundation.org.

SECOND SATURDAYS ON THE WINE TRAIL

Second Saturday One-Price Tasting Special. Stop by any trail member's tasting room on the second Saturday of the month and purchase your trail wristband for fifteen dollars. The wristband is good for that day and entitles you to a standard tasting at up to five trail member stops. Wristbands are not refundable and non-transferrable. You must be twenty-one with photo ID.

TABLE AND VINE EXPO

Typically held in the middle of May in West Springfield, Massachusetts, the expo usually features many Hudson Valley producers.

WINE AND FOOD FESTIVAL (MEMORIAL DAY)

The Hudson-Berkshire Wine and Food Festival is held annually on Memorial Day at the Columbia Country Fairgrounds in Chatham, New York.

SHAWANGUNK WINE TRAIL

Events

BOUNTY OF THE HUDSON

Held at Ulster County Fairgrounds in New Paltz, New York, annually in June, this two-day wine and food festival celebrates the wines of the Hudson Valley, fresh local produce and epicurean treats from local restaurants. Live music is also featured.

Appendix C

Hudson Valley Wine Tasting Passport

Valid January 1–August 31. With the Hudson Valley Wine Tasting Passport, you may visit each of the fifteen wineries of the Shawangunk Wine Trail at your own pace. Visit one or more wineries at a time. Your passport allows you to visit each winery once and receive a full tasting at each one. You have a full eight months to visit all the wineries.

Wreath Fineries at the Wineries

The self-guided wine tasting tour features shopping opportunities with local artisans along the Shawangunk Wine Trail. Participants pick the weekend date (late November through December) and a winery for their starting point. The event begins with check-in at your starting winery, where participants receive a souvenir wine glass, a grapevine wreath and a Shawangunk Wine Trail ornament (a couple's ticket shares the wreath and ornament). Then you get to travel along the wine trail, receiving a wine tasting and a beautiful ornament to decorate your wreath from each winery you visit.

TASTE NY LOCATIONS

Albany International Airport
Address: Albany Shaker Road, Colonie, NY 12110
Phone: (518) 242-2200
Taste NY kiosks offer travelers locally made cheese, healthy snacks, maple candy and drinks.

Angola Travel Paza
Address: 447 I-90, Angola, NY 14006
Phone: (716) 549-3605
Taste NY kiosks at NYS Thruway service areas offer travelers locally made cheese, healthy snacks, maple candy and drinks.

Buffalo Niagara International Airport
Address: 4200 Genesee Street, Buffalo, NY 14225
Phone: (716) 630-6000
Taste NY kiosks offer travelers locally made cheese, healthy snacks, maple candy and drinks.

Cave of the Winds Pavilion Plaza
Prospect Street and Old Falls Street, Niagara Falls, NY 14303
A selection of Taste NY products at the Cave of the Winds Gift Shop at Niagara Falls State Park. Hours vary by season.

Chittenango Travel Plaza
New York State Thruway, Chittenango, NY 13037
Phone: (315) 687-0015
This Taste NY kiosk at the Chittenango Service Area on the NYS Thruway
is open twenty-four hours.

DeWitt Travel Plaza
De Witt, NY 13206
Taste NY kiosks at NYS Thruway service areas offer travelers locally made
cheese, healthy snacks, maple candy and drinks.

Empire State Plaza Visitors Center
Address: 100 South Mall Arterial, Albany, NY 12210
Phone: (518) 474-2418
The Taste NY store at the Empire State Plaza in Albany is open weekdays
8:30 a.m.–4:30 p.m. and shares space with I LOVE NY products.

The Glen Iris Inn
Address: 7 Letchworth State Park, Castile, NY 14427
Phone: (585) 493-2622
Taste NY products are featured at the Glen Iris Inn in Letchworth State
Park. Hours vary by season.

Grand Central Station
89 East Forty-Second Street, New York, NY 10017
A full-fledged Taste NY store is now open at the Grand Central Terminal in
New York City (across from track 37).

Guilderland Travel Plaza
Adress: 103 Brookview Drive, Schenectady, NY 12303
Phone: (518) 357-0308
Taste NY kiosks at NYS Thruway service areas offer travelers locally made
cheese, healthy snacks, maple candy and drinks.

Jones Beach State Park
Address: 1 Ocean Parkway, Wantagh, NY 11793
Phone: (516) 785-1600
The Taste NY Café at Jones Beach State Park is open May through
September 5.

Letchworth State Park
Address: Castile, NY 14427
Phone: (585) 493-3600
The Gift Shop at Letchworth State Park will offer a selection of Taste NY products. Hours vary by season.

Lock E-13 Living History Park
NYS Thruway 90 West
Address: Fultonville, NY 12072
The Taste NY store off the NYS Thruway westbound at exit 28 offers goods from thirty New York–based producers.

MacArthur Airport
Address: 100 Arrival Avenue, Ronkonkoma, NY 11779
Phone: (631) 467-3300
The Taste NY shop is in the East End Getaway boutique at Long Island MacArthur Airport and offers local wine and food products.

Malden Travel Plaza
Address: Saugerties, NY 12477
Phone: (845) 246-7670
Taste NY kiosks at NYS Thruway service areas offer travelers locally made cheese, healthy snacks, maple candy and drinks.

Modena Travel Plaza
Address: Milepost 66 Southbound, Modena, NY 12548
Phone: (845) 566-4056
Taste NY kiosks at NYS Thruway service areas offer travelers locally made cheese, healthy snacks, maple candy and drinks.

Mohawk Travel Plaza
Address: 276 Service Road, Amsterdam, NY 12010
Taste NY kiosks at NYS Thruway service areas offer travelers locally made cheese, healthy snacks, maple candy and drinks.

New Baltimore Travel Plaza
Address: 127 New York State Thruway, Hannacroix, NY 12087
Phone: (518) 756-3000
The Taste NY store at New Baltimore Service Area on the NYS Thruway is located just south of Albany.

Nikon Amphitheater
The Taste NY bar at Nikon Amphitheater at Jones Beach State Park.

Ontario Travel Plaza
Address: Governor Thomas E. Dewey Thruway, New York, NY 14482
Phone: (585) 293-3750
Taste NY kiosks at NYS Thruway service areas offer travelers locally made cheese, healthy snacks, maple candy and drinks.

Pattersonville Service Area
Address: New York State Thruway, Mile Post 168 West, Pattersonville, NY 12137
Phone: (518) 887-2028
This is the first stand-alone store on the NYS Thruway and is located westbound I-90 between exit 26 and exit 27.

Port Byron Travel Plaza
Address: Milepost 310 Eastbound, Port Byron, NY 13140
Phone: (315) 776-5700
Taste NY kiosks at NYS Thruway service areas offer travelers locally made cheese, healthy snacks, maple candy and drinks.

Ramapo Travel Plaza
Address: Milepost 33 Southbound, Sloatsburg, NY 10974
Phone: (845) 753-2073
Taste NY kiosks at NYS Thruway service areas offer travelers locally made cheese, healthy snacks, maple candy and drinks.

Schuyler Travel Plaza
Address: 265 Carder Lane Road, Frankfort, NY 13340
Phone: (315) 894-4211
Taste NY kiosks at NYS Thruway service areas offer travelers locally made cheese, healthy snacks, maple candy and drinks.

Sloatsburg Service Area
The Sloatsburg store is located on I-87 northbound between exit 15A and exit 16 and is open twenty-four hours.

State Fair Taste NY Marketplace
Address: New York State Fairgrounds, 581 State Fair Boulevard, Syracuse, NY 13209
The Taste NY Marketplace is located at the New York State Fairgrounds.

Syracuse Hancock International Airport
Address: 1000 Col Eileen Collins Boulevard, Syracuse, NY 13212
Phone: (315) 454-4330
Taste NY kiosks offer travelers locally made cheese, healthy snacks, maple candy and drinks.

Taste NY Café at Whiteface Mountain
Address: 5021 Route 86, Wilmington, NY 12997
Phone: (518) 946-2174
This brand-new agri-tourism attraction provides visitors the opportunity to try some of the best local food and beverages.

Todd Hill Rest Area
Address: Taconic State Parkway, Lagrangeville, NY 12540
Phone: (845) 849-0247
The Taste NY Market is located at the Todd Hill rest area on the Taconic Parkway (one mile south of Route 55).

Top of the Falls Restaurant
Address: 24 Buffalo Avenue, Niagara Falls, NY 14303
Phone: (716) 278-0340
Taste NY products are featured in the menu at the Top of the Falls restaurant on Goat Island at Niagara Falls State Park.

Warners Travel Plaza
Address: 2660 Brickyard Road, Warners, NY 13164
Phone: (315) 672-3951
Taste NY kiosks at NYS Thruway service areas offer travelers locally made cheese, healthy snacks, maple candy and drinks.

Watkins Glen State Park
Address: 1009 North Franklin Street, Watkins Glen, NY 14891
Phone: (607) 535-4511
A selection of Taste NY products are showcased at the Main Gift Shop at Watkins Glen State Park. Hours vary by season.

HISTORIC HUDSON VALLEY HOMES

*T*hese homes are just some of the examples of the stunning historical landmarks that seem to hide behind every corner in the Hudson Valley. Many offer tours and have sprawling grounds to explore.

1. BOSCOBEL (Garrison)
Boscobel is a sprawling estate built in the early nineteenth century overlooking the Hudson River.
Address: 1601 Route 9D, Garrison, NY 10524
Phone: (845) 265-3638
boscobel.org

2. CLERMONT (Germantown)
Clermont State Historic Site is home to one of New York's most politically and socially prominent dynasties: the Livingston family. Seven successive generations of the family left their imprint on the site's architecture, room interiors and landscape. Robert R. Livingston Jr. was Clermont's most notable resident.
Address: 1 Clermont Avenue (off Route 9G), Germantown, NY 12526
Phone: (518) 537-4240
friendsofclermont.org

3. CLINTON HOUSE
The Clinton House is a historic building located in downtown Ithaca, New York. It is built primarily in the Greek Revival style, common in older buildings in Ithaca.
Address: 549 Main Street, Poughkeepsie, NY 12866
Phone: (845) 471-1630

4. DR. OLIVER BRONSON HOUSE
The Plumb-Bronson House, also known as the Dr. Oliver Bronson House and Stables, is a historic landmark in Hudson, New York. The house was originally built for Samuel Plumb, who purchased the site in 1811.
Address: Hudson, NY 12534
Phone: (518) 828-1785

5. FRANKLIN D. ROOSEVELT HISTORIC SITE
The Home of Franklin D. Roosevelt National Historic Site preserves the Springwood estate in Hyde Park, New York. Springwood was the birthplace, lifelong home and burial place of President Franklin Delano Roosevelt.
Address: 4097 Albany Post Road, Hyde Park, NY 12538
Phone: (845) 229-9115

6. GLENVIEW (Yonkers)
Glenview Mansion, listed in the National Register of Historic Places as the John Bond Trevor House, is located on Warburton Avenue in Yonkers, New York.
Address: 511 Warburton Avenue, Yonkers, NY 10701
Phone: (914) 963-4550
hrm.org

7. GRAHAM-BRUSH LOG HOUSE
Graham-Brush Log House is a historic home located at the hamlet of Pine Plains in the town of Pine Plains, Dutchess County, New York. It was built in about 1776 and is a two-room log structure with a wood frame lean-to on its rear elevation.
Address: 5932 North Union Road, Pine Plains, NY 12567

8. JAMES VANDERPOOL HOUSE
The James Vanderpool House in Kinderhook was built around 1819 for a prominent lawyer and politician. The brick home is considered a stunning example of Federal style.

Address: 16 Broad Street, Kinderhook, NY 12106
Phone: (518) 758-9265

9. Jan Van Hosesen House
Jan Van Hoesen House is an early eighteenth-century house in New York State. Between Hudson and Chatham, just east of Claverack Creek, this home stands as sentinel over the Dutch Acres Mobile Home Park.
Address: Sabo Lane, Hudson NY 12534 on the north side of Route 66

10. Kykuit (Sleepy Hollow)
Kykuit, known also as the John D. Rockefeller Estate, is a fifty-room National Trust house in Westchester County, New York, built by order of oil tycoon and Rockefeller family patriarch John D. Rockefeller.
Address: Phillipsburg Manor, Route 9, Sleepy Hollow, NY 10591
Phone: (914) 631-8200
hudsonvalley.org/content/view/12/42

11. Langdon Estate Gatehouse
The Langdon Estate Gatehouse is located in Hyde Park. It was built in 1876 and is a one-and-a-half-story, two-bay dwelling in the Renaissance Revival style.
Address: 4419 Albany Post Road, Hyde Park, NY 12538

12. Lindenwald (Kinderhook)
Martin Van Buren National Historic Site is a unit of the United States National Park Service located twenty miles south of Albany. The home of the former president features walking trails as well.
Address: 1013 Old Post Road, Kinderhook, NY 12106
Phone: (518) 758-968
www.nps.gov/mava

13. Locust Grove (Poughkeepsie)
Locust Grove is a National Historic Landmark estate in Poughkeepsie.
Address: 370 South Road (Route 9), PO Box 1649, Poughkeepsie, NY 12601
Phone: (845) 454-4500
lgny.org

14. Luykas Van Alen House
The Van Alen House or Luykas Van Alen House is a historic Dutch brick farmhouse built in approximately 1737.

Address: 2589 Route 9H, Kinderhook, NY 12106
Phone: (518) 758-9265

15. LYNDHURST (Tarrytown)
Lyndhurst, also known as the Jay Gould estate, is a Gothic Revival country
house that sits in its own sixty-seven-acre park beside the Hudson River in
Tarrytown.
Address: 635 South Broadway, Tarrytown, NY 10591
Phone: (914) 631-4481
lyndhurst.org

16. MONTGOMERY PLACE (Annandale-on-Hudson)
An early nineteenth-century estate that has been designated a National
Historic Landmark.
Address: River Road, off Route 9G, Annandale-on-Hudson, NY 12571
Phone: (845) 758-5461, or contact Historic Hudson Valley at (914) 631-8200
hudsonvalley.org/content/view/16/46/

17. OLANA (Hudson)
Olana State Historic Site was the home of Frederic Edwin Church, one of
the major figures in the Hudson River School of landscape painting.
Address: RD 2, Route 9G, Hudson, NY 12534
Phone: (518) 828-0135
olana.org

18. PHILIPSBURG MANOR, UPPER MILLS (Sleepy Hollow)
Philipsburg Manor is a seventeenth-century historic site dedicated to telling
the story of slavery in the colonial North.
Address: Route 9, Sleepy Hollow, NY 10591
Phone: (914) 631-8200
hudsonvalley.org/content/view/14/44

19. ROBERT JENKINS HOUSE
The Robert Jenkins House was built in 1811 by Robert Jenkins, the third
and fifth mayor of Hudson and the son of original Hudson proprietor
Seth Jenkins.
Address: 113 Warren Street, Hudson, NY 12534

20. STAATSBURGH (Mills Mansion in Staatsburgh)
The Staatsburgh State Historic Site preserves a Beaux-Arts mansion designed by McKim, Mead and White and the home's surrounding landscape.
Address: Old Post Road, Staatsburg, NY 12580
Phone: (845) 889-8851

21. SUNNYSIDE (Tarrytown)
Sunnyside is a historic house on ten acres along the Hudson River in Tarrytown, New York. It was the home of the noted American author Washington Irving, best known for his short stories.
Address: Tarrytown, NY 10591
Phone: (914) 591-8763 or contact Historic Hudson Valley at (914) 631-8200
hudsonvalley.org/content/view/13/43/

22. VAL-KILL (Hyde Park)
Eleanor Roosevelt National Historic Site preserves the Stone Cottage at Val-Kill, the home of First Lady Eleanor Roosevelt, and its surrounding property of 181 acres.
Address: 519 Albany Post Road, Hyde Park, NY 12538
Phone: (845) 229-9115
nps.gov/elro

23. VAN CORTLANDT MANOR (Croton-on-Hudson)
Van Cortlandt Manor is a house and property located by the confluence of the Croton and Hudson Rivers located in the village of Croton-on-Hudson in Westchester County, New York.
Address: Riverside Avenue, Croton-on-Hudson, NY 10520
Phone: (914) 271-8981 or contact Historic Hudson Valley at (914) 631-8200
hudsonvalley.org/content/view/15/45

24. VANDERBILT MANSION (Hyde Park)
Vanderbilt Mansion National Historic Site, located in Hyde Park, New York, is one of America's premier examples of the country palaces built by wealthy industrialists during the Gilded Age.
Address: 519 Albany Post Road, Hyde Park, NY 12538
Phone: (845) 229-9115
nps.gov/vama

25. WILDERSTEIN (Rhinebeck)

Wilderstein is a nineteenth-century Queen Anne–style country house on the Hudson River in Rhinebeck, Dutchess County, New York.
Address: Morton Road, PO Box 383, Rhinebeck, NY 12572
Phone: (845) 876-4818
wilderstein.org

WINE, RESTAURANT AND HISTORIC SITES ITINERARIES

*T*here are so many routes to take through beautiful Hudson Valley wine country. Here are a few of our favorite day trips, with stops at wineries, restaurants and historic sites.

ROUTE RHINEBECK AND SOUTH

Rhinebeck is a town in Dutchess County, New York. It is in the Poughkeepsie-Newburgh-Middletown region.

Wilderstein

Wilderstein is located on the Hudson River in Rhinebeck. It is a nineteenth-century Queen Anne–style country house.
Address: 330 Morton Road, Rhinebeck, NY 12572
Phone: (845) 876-4818

Franklin D. Roosevelt Home

The Franklin D. Roosevelt National Historic Site is an estate in Hyde Park, New York. The president was born, raised and buried in Springwood.
Address: 4097 Albany Post Road, Hyde Park, NY 12538
Phone: (845) 229-9115

Vanderbilt Mansion National Historic Site

Vanderbilt Mansion National Historic Site is located in Hyde Park, New York. It is a palace in the countryside built by rich manufacturers during the Gilded Age.
Address: 119 Vanderbilt Park Road, Hyde Park, NY 12538
Phone: (845) 229-7770

Clinton Vineyards

Clinton Vineyards is a creative yet traditional place with estate-bottled wines. It is known as "the jewel in the crown of the Hudson Valley." The wine selection (Gold Award winning) includes Seyval single-grape vintages, sparkling and dessert wines.
Address: 450 Schultzville Road, Clinton Corners, NY 12514
Phone: (845) 266-5372

Roundhouse at Beacon

The Roundhouse by Terrance Brennan is passionately committed to sustainability and supporting local farms, wineries, distilleries, cideries and all of the amazing food and beverage craftsmen of the Hudson Valley.
Address: 2 East Main Street, Beacon, NY 12508
Phone: (845) 765-8369

Poets' Walk

This includes almost two miles of trails of meadows and woods. In addition, the Overlook Pavilion, a rustic summer house with benches, provides a beautiful rest stop along the trail.
Address: 776 River Road, Red Hook, NY 12571
Phone: (845) 473-4440

Robibero Winery

Address: 714 Albany Post Road, New Paltz, NY 12561
Phone: (845) 255-9463

Village Tea Room

A locally sourced and organic American tearoom in a charming and comfortable historic building.
Address: 10 Plattekill Avenue, New Paltz, NY 12561
Phone: (845) 255-3434

Adair Vineyards

Adair Vineyards is located in the historic Hudson Valley, where wine growing and importing/exporting has been popular for quite some time.
Address: 52 Allhusen Road, New Paltz, NY 12561
Phone: (845) 255-1377

Huguenot Street Historic District

Historic Huguenot Street is located in New Paltz, New York, where the streets are famously lined with beautiful stone houses. It is only a couple hours from New York City.
Address: 81 Huguenot Street, New Paltz, NY
Phone: (845) 255-1889

Mohonk Preserve

The Mohonk Preserve is New York's most popular nature preserve. Every year, around 165,000 visitors come to see the eight thousand acres of cliffs, forests, fields, ponds and streams.
Address: 3197 US-44, Gardiner, NY 12525
Phone: (845) 255-0919

Minnewaska State Park Preserve

The Minnewaska State Park Preserve is a 22,275-acre preserve. You can find this beautiful site at Shawangunk Ridge in Ulster County, New York.
Address: 5281 Route 44-55, Kerhonkson, NY 12446
Phone: (845) 255-0752

Route Saratoga Springs and West

Saratoga Springs is located in Saratoga County, New York, a small city that offers the charms of the country and the convenience and culture of a larger metropolitan area.

Salt & Char

Salt & Char is a delicious restaurant that cooks with the goal of supporting local farmers with organic and sustainable practices.
Address: 353 Broadway, Saratoga Springs, NY 12866
Phone: (518) 450-7500

15 Church

15 Church was originally a historic building, but it has been converted into a restaurant in downtown Saratoga Springs, New York. The restaurant provides fresh seafood daily. Its menu is ever changing and artistic, and the ambiance is stylish and calm.
Address: 15 Church Street, Saratoga Springs, NY 12866
Phone: (518) 587-1515

The Saratoga Winery

Address: 462 NY-29, Saratoga Springs, NY 12866
Phone: (518) 584-9463

Thirsty Owl

The Thirsty Owl offers wine from Cayuga Lake vineyards and new American food.
Address: 184 South Broadway, Saratoga Springs, NY 12866
Phone: (518) 587-9694

Saratoga Race Course

Saratoga Race Course is a thoroughbred horse racing track located in Saratoga Springs. The racetrack can hold up to fifty thousand people.
Address: 267 Union Avenue, Saratoga Springs, NY 12866
Phone: (718) 641-4700

Skidmore College

Skidmore College is a private, independent liberal arts college in Saratoga Springs, New York. Approximately 2,500 students are enrolled at Skidmore pursuing a bachelor of arts or bachelor of science degree in one of more than sixty areas of study.
Address: 815 North Broadway, Saratoga Springs, NY 12866
Phone: (518) 580-5000

Saratoga Spa State Park

Saratoga Spa State Park covers 2,379 acres of land; with beautiful playing fields, historic buildings, forest trails and hidden springs, there is something for everyone.
Address: 19 Roosevelt Drive, Saratoga Springs, NY 12866
Phone: (518) 584-2535

Congress Park

Canfield Casino and Congress Park covers seventeen acres of land in Saratoga Springs and used to be where the Congress Spring Bottling Plant and the Congress Hall was located.
Address: East Congress Street, Saratoga Springs, NY 12866

ROUTE HUDSON AND NORTH

Hudson is an artsy city with a chic vibe located along the west side of Columbia County.

Olana State Historic Site

Olana State Historic Site was home to Frederic Edwin Church. He was an important influence in the Hudson River School of landscape painting.
Address: 5720 State Route 9G, Hudson, NY 12534

Hudson-Chatham Winery

The Hudson-Chatham Winery was Columbia County's first winery. In 2006, the two proud owners transformed their fourteen acres of land from a dairy farm to a winery and tasting room.

Address: 1900 NY-66, Ghent, NY 12075
Phone: (518) 392-9463

Millbrook Vineyards and Winery

Millbrook Vineyards and Winery is thirty-five acres of vines. The vineyard includes Pinot Noir, Chardonnay, Cabernet Franc, Riesling and Tocai Friulano.
Address: 26 Wing Road, Millbrook, NY 12545
Phone: (845) 677-8383

Tousey Winery

Address: 1774 Route 9, Germantown, NY 12526
Phone: (518) 567-5462

Bartlett House

This bakery and café provides house-made bread, baked goods, breakfast/brunch, prepared food and sandwiches with weekend dinners.
Address: 2258 State Route 66, Ghent, NY 12075
Phone: (518) 392-7787

Clermont State Historic Site

The Clermont State Historic Site is also known as the Clermont estate. It is a New York State Historic Site in Columbia County, New York.
Address: 1 Clermont Avenue, Germantown, NY 12526
Phone: (518) 537-4240

The Maker

This unique boutique hotel is home to the Bartlett House bakers and is a mecca for local food and wine experiences in the Hudson Valley in a unique historic setting on Warren Street.
Address: Corner of Third and Warren Streets, Hudson, NY 12534
Phone: (518) 392-7787

Montgomery Place (at Bard College)

The Montgomery Place Campus is a nineteenth-century estate designated as a National Historic Landmark. Architect Alexander Jackson Davis designed the Federal-style house. He was part of the post-Revolutionary generation of rich landowners. His design was influenced by French trends seen in home design, moving forward and past the strict English models seen in other manors near by. It is Davis's only surviving neoclassical work.

Oliva Vineyards

At Oliva Vineyards, wine, horse racing and family come together.
Address: 240 Excelsior Avenue, Saratoga Springs, NY 12866
Phone: (518) 350-4515

Fish & Game

Awarded, celebrated and committed to local food and libations, James Beard award–winning chef Zakary Pelaccio is living the practice of sustainability with organic and hand-crafted products with his wife, Chef Jori Jayne Emde, and her apothecary of alchemy-based products called Lady Jayne's Alchemy, crafted with skilled hands from their garden.
Address: 13 South Third Street, Hudson, NY 12534
Phone: (518) 822-1500

Spotty Dog Books & Ale

This bookstore is proud to carry over ten thousand new books in many various categories. It has books and toys for kids and adolescents and books on the local area, history, gardening, food and wine. The owners are proud to provide both classic and cutting-edge pieces and constantly are adding to their collections.
Address: 440 Warren Street, Hudson, NY 12534
Phone: (518) 671-6006

GETTING AROUND

Want to go but don't want to drive (for obvious reasons)? These are the three go-to options for safe rides.

THE LITTLE WINE BUS

This tour company departs many weekends from Midtown Manhattan and journeys to the Hudson Valley on various wine- and beer-themed excursions. Also available for private rental.
(917) 414-7949
thelittlewinebus.com

ALL STAR LIMO

This organization holds wine tours around the Hudson Valley, with a variety of options for itineraries and stops along the way.
(800) 546-6669
allstarlimo.com

ALL TRANSPORTATION NETWORK

All Trans offers everything from limo service to full-size motor coaches for
your own custom-designed itinerary.
(800) 525-2306
alltrans.net

SOURCES

Books

Bedford, Robert. *The Story of Brotherhood: America's Oldest Winery*. Coxsackie, NY: Flint Mine Press, 2014.

Casscles, J. Stephen. *Grapes of the Hudson Valley: Other Cool Climate Regions of the Unites States and Canada*. Coxsackie, NY: Flint Mine Press, 2015.

McGovern, Patrick. *The Quest for Wine, Beer and Other Alcoholic Beverages*. Berkeley: University of California Press, 2010.

Rosenthal, Neal I. *Reflections of a Wine Merchant*. New York: North Point Press, 2009.

Articles

Casscles, J. Stephen. "Keeping It Currant." *Hudson Valley Wine*. http://www.hvwinemag.com/Grapes_currant.html.

Franson, Paul. "Number of United States Wineries Reaches 8,702." *Wine Business Monthly*, February 2016. https://www.winebusiness.com/wbm/?go=getArticleSignIn&dataId=163894.

Willcox, Kathleen. "Distilling a Revolution." *Hudson Valley Wine*. http://www.hvwinemag.com/features_distilling.html.

———. "Vines of the Times." *Hudson Valley Wine*. http://www.hvwinemag.com/features_vines.html.

Wine Institute. "U.S. Wine, Grapes and Grape Products Contribute $162 Billion to U.S. Economy." PRNewswire. Last modified January 17, 2007. http://www.prnewswire.com/news-releases/us-wine-grapes-and-grape-products-contribute-162-billion-to-economy-53562372.html.

Zavatto, Amy. "Can We Be Franc?" *Hudson Valley Wine*, Summer 2016. https://issuu.com/hvwinemagazine/docs/hvw_summer2016_issuu.

Studies and Online Resources

Creative Feed. "Generation Wine: Distinguishing Millennials and Boomers in Today's Wine Culture." http://www.creativefeed.net/generation-wine.

Glynwood. "The State of Agriculture in the Hudson Valley." https://glynwood.org/wp-content/uploads/2015/02/State-of-Agriculture-2010.pdf.

Hudson Valley Wine & Grape Association. "The Roots of American Wine Since 1677's Index of Grapes." Hudson Valley Wine Country. http://www.hudsonvalleywinecountry.org/grapes.html.

———. "The Roots of American Wine Since 1677's Wine Trails List." Hudson Valley Wine Country. http://www.hudsonvalleywinecountry.org/wine-trails.html.

National Cooperative Soil Series. "Hudson Series." https://soilseries.sc.egov.usda.gov/OSD_Docs/H/HUDSON.html.

New York Wines. www.newyorkwines.org.

Saratoga Zymurgist. "Apple Pie Mead Recipe." http://saratogaz.com/Apple-Pie-Mead_ep_77.html.

Stonebridge Research. "Economic Impact of Napa County's Wine and Grapes." https://napavintners.com/community/docs/napa_economic_impact_2012.pdf.

VinePair. "The Yellow Tail Story: How Two Families Turned Australia into America's Biggest Wine Brand." http://vinepair.com/wine-blog/how-yellow-tail-gave-america-australian-wine/.

Wine Cellar Insider. "French Wine Classifications AOC Law." http://www.thewinecellarinsider.com/wine-topics/wine-educational-questions/wine-grapes-vineyard-france-classifications-appellation-law.

Wine Searcher. "Brand Is King in North America." http://www.wine-searcher.com/m/2013/07/wine-giants-monopolize-american-market.

INDEX

ABOUT THE AUTHORS

TESSA EDICK is a journalist, author, school food activist, philanthropist, food entrepreneur, executive director and founder of the FarmOn! Foundation, a 501(c)3 nonprofit organization and public charity that created a grass-roots movement to change food and inspire youth education in agriculture. Edick launched her career in the food industry and revolutionized ready-made tomato sauce in a jar sourcing from the farm, garnering over two hundred print and television impressions as it grew globally, including two features in the *Oprah* magazine "O" list, as well as sixteen SFT "Sofi" awards. Edick's first book, *Hudson Valley Food and Farming: Why Didn't Anyone Tell Me That?*, was published in 2014. Edick writes a bimonthly column, "Meet Your Farmer," and produces content for the national quarterly *Modern Farmer*. In 2016, Edick was appointed by Governor Andrew Cuomo to the task force on Safe and Healthy Food and in 2015 by executive order to the NYS Council on Food Policy. She serves on the Advisory Board for Edible Schoolyard by mentor Alice Waters. She resides in Copake Lake, New York, with her partner, a twelve-year NBA veteran of the Boston Celtics, and an English bulldog and an English mastiff, Ms. Ruby Juice and Lady Trudie Astor, respectively.

KATHLEEN WILLCOX is a journalist who writes about food, wine, beer and popular culture; her work has appeared in *Edible: Capital District*, *Edible: Green Mountains*, *Hudson Valley Wine* magazine and *VinePair*; on United Stations Radio Network; and in many other media. She lives in Saratoga Springs with her husband, Stephen Repsher, and their young twins, Emily and Miles.

Visit us at
www.historypress.net
....
This title is also available as an e-book